Happy Holidays!
from Tri-Aegis, Inc.
December 1994

Reflections for Managers

Reflections for Managers

Bruce N. Hyland
Merle J. Yost

McGraw-Hill, Inc.

New York San Francisco Washington, D.C. Auckland Bogotá
Caracas Lisbon London Madrid Mexico City Milan
Montreal New Delhi San Juan Singapore
Sydney Tokyo Toronto

Library of Congress Cataloging-in-Publication Data

Hyland, Bruce.
    Reflections for managers / Bruce Hyland, Merle Yost.
        p.   cm.
    ISBN 0-07-031739-9
    1. Industrial management .   2. Psychology, Industrial.   I. Yost,
Merle. II. Title.
    HD31.H95 1993   93-29242
    658—dc20   CIP

    3 4 5 6 7 8 9 0 DOH/DOH 9 9 8 7 6 5 4

ISBN 0-07-031739-9

The sponsoring editor for this book was James H. Bessent, Jr., the editing supervisor was Kimberly A. Goff, and the production supervisor was Suzanne W. Babeuf. This book was designed and set in Palatino by Susan Maksuta on a MacIntosh system.

Printed and bound by R. R. Donnelley & Sons Company.

*To our mentors and
guides along the way,
particularly those who told us
to celebrate with pink balloons.*

Contents

Sensitivity

1. Caring Produces Results   2
2. Realize: To Most People, It's Only a Job   4
3. Honor Differences   6
4. Say Thank You   8
5. Ask Your Employees What They Need   10
6. Loyalty Begets Loyalty   12
7. Admit When You Are Wrong…and Quickly   14
8. Authority Must Equal Responsibility   16

Company Politics

9. Management Is an Artificial Role   20
10. Don't Hitch Your Wagon to Anyone Else's Star   22
11. Choose Your Words Carefully   24
12. Know Your Obligations   26
13. Take Time to Read the Environment   28
14. Contacts Are Gold   30
15. Don't Burn Your Bridges   32

Leadership

16. You Are Responsible for Your Feelings and Actions   36
17. Don't Put Yourself on a Pedestal   38
18. Study Is Not a Substitute for Timely Decision Making   40

19. Be Visible — 42
20. Deal with It or Live with It — 44
21. Stay the Course — 46
22. Finish What You Start — 48
23. Adopt a Code of Conduct — 50
24. Know How Your Employees Think — 52

The Big Picture

25. Keep the Big Picture in Mind — 56
26. Few Decisions Are Forever — 58
27. Examine Your Perceptions — 60
28. You Won't Always Win — 62
29. Know Why Your Organization Exists — 64
30. There Are Few "Right" Answers — 66
31. Embrace Quality — 68
32. One Battle Does Not Make a War — 70
33. Don't Always Expect a Happy Ending — 72

Team Building

34. Know Your Working Style — 76
35. Know Your Team Members — 78
36. Define Roles Clearly — 80
37. Make Requests Instead of Issuing Orders — 82
38. Provide Feedback, Both Formally and Informally — 84
39. Reward Good People and Good Performance — 86
40. Celebrate Success — 88

The Day to Day

41. Leave the Old Job Behind   92
42. Know the Real Organizational Chart   94
43. Set Up Systems   96
44. Find and Deal with the Real Problem   98
45. You Have Choices   100
46. Cultivate a Personal Support System   102
47. Don't Be Afraid to Ask for Help   104
48. Just Say No   106

Technique

49. Know the History of Your Organization   110
50. Vision Must Be Supported by Action   112
51. Stay in Touch   114
52. Listen for the Unspoken   116
53. Learn to Disagree Without Being Disagreeable   118
54. Hold People to Their Commitments   120
55. Be Diplomatic Without Sacrificing the Message   122
56. Handle Employee Problems Promptly   124
57. Terminate When Necessary   126

Image

58. Appearance Really Does Count   130
59. Sex and Work Don't Mix   132
60. Take Care of Yourself   134
61. Fit in, but Don't Be Invisible   136

62. You Are Not Perfect   138
63. Superior Management Requires Professional Development   140
64. Always Do Well   142

Preface

Two major influences sparked the decision to write this book. One was our own education in the corporate environment and how to thrive in it.

As we, the authors, ventured forth into the business world to succeed and conquer, we encountered a world for which we were not prepared. It was a world apart from school and the relative safety of our parents' homes. There were rules and expectations everyone seemed to know that were not so obvious to us. Fortunately, we were each taken in hand by mentors who showed us the ropes and guided our early endeavors. We worked with and learned from some great managers and leaders (and some who were not so great, but from whom we also learned). Without this guidance the journey would have been much more difficult, if not impossible.

It's possible to learn a lot about being a manager from formal textbooks, courses, and lectures. However, the best teacher is hands-on experience. In looking back at our education, we both have often wished for a book that explained some of the basic principles of leadership, management, and dealing with people in real-life situations.

The other influence was the education of our employees, particularly the ones we hired to be managers, who had little or no experience. In our years of management, we have done extensive hiring and training. In our consulting practices, we have worked with other executives and managers who faced similar issues. We have had to take new employees who have never worked for a large company and quickly educate and make them productive members of the work force. We have had to turn them into managers and educate them on the basics of management and people skills. We have had to take managers and make them manage better. The principles apply across the board. Part of our coming together to write this book was an attempt to document these basic principles of management.

A lot of discussion of these experiences led us to document the management and leadership rules that have evolved for us over the years. To add to our experience, we met informally with hundreds of mid- and top-management people through Chambers of Commerce, professional associations, and workshops. We also met with top managers in nonprofit settings and government. To balance our findings and to see if there were any dramatic differences in perceptions, we met with hundreds of employees in focus groups and adult business education classes. Feeling that it was important to validate our informal research, we decided to conduct a more formal survey, and contacted CEOs and presidents of major corporations, asking for their top ten rules of management and leadership.

The top managers, mid-managers, and employees' "rules for managers" were incredibly similar—both in profit and nonprofit arenas. The universal foundation was a focus on people and people skills. *Listen, listen, listen* was stated over and over. *Talk to people, know how they feel, know what they want, and communicate, communicate, communicate.* These strong themes emerged. We are hopeful that this book helps to communicate some of the basic principles of management and leadership.

We are extremely grateful for the time and effort of all those who responded. The following are the respondents who were particularly generous with their feedback in the surveys they returned (we regret that we cannot list everyone who contributed to this project): C. Fretterolf, President, ALCOA, Pittsburgh, PA; J. Moseley, President,

USF&G Corp., Baltimore, MD; Kenneth Macke, CEO, Dayton Hudson, Minneapolis, MN; Philip Dion, President, Del Webb Corp., Phoenix, AZ; Hugh Aycock, President, Nucor Corp., Charlotte, NC; Dave Fox, President, Northern Trust, Chicago, IL; Ralph Reins, CEO, Mack Trucks, Inc., Allentown, PA; R. Erben, President, Luby's Cafeterias, San Antonio, TX; and Robert Krebs, President, Santa Fe Pacific, Chicago, IL.

Bruce N. Hyland
Merle J. Yost

Sensitivity

1

CARING PRODUCES RESULTS

People won't care how much you know until they know how much you care. Communicate your concern for people first, then you can ask them to do anything.

In More Depth

People respond when someone sincerely cares about them. This doesn't mean giving them whatever they want. It does mean taking a personal interest and treating them with respect.

We are not a society of robots. We work with people. People have feelings. Everyone wants to be liked, appreciated, and respected. Treated this way, they respond much more favorably and enthusiastically. Treated like robots, they respond like robots. You may get your specified output, but you will rarely get any creativity or dramatic improvements. When poorly treated, employees' unhappiness tends to come out in covert ways, such as low morale and personnel problems.

A cautionary note, however. Sincerity is critical. It is worse to fake it. Your people can read you. If you're insincere, they'll not only feel you don't care but also that you are trying to trick them.

The Idea in Action

Charles E. was chairman of the chemistry department of a state university. He was more comfortable with research than with personnel issues, but he knew that, as chairman, working with people was now a primary component of his job.

Dr. E. was not a particularly strong personality. He was soft-spoken and scholarly. Yet, over the years he had firmly established himself as a respected leader in the department, and throughout the entire school.

Other chairmen around campus didn't quite understand his secret. When they asked, he would just scratch his head and shrug, saying, "I don't know either. I have a great group of people. I'm just lucky they are so talented and so willing to work with me. "

Then one year, Dr. E's name came up among nominees for best administrator. When the vice president of academic affairs went to interview people in the department, he found one very interesting theme: Dr. E. cared about his people. He listened to them, even if he couldn't agree or grant their requests. He would advocate their concerns to the administration. He would pay attention to their personal interests and would always show kindness and understanding when someone had marital problems, an illness, or a death in the family.

His staff said that while Dr. E. was not particularly dynamic, they would rather have a caring leader who was competent than a dynamo who didn't care about them. They liked working for him and they pulled together because "they wanted him to succeed."

Dr. E. didn't win the award that year, but he continued to win "silent awards" from his staff and experience the satisfaction of managing an effective and pleasant team.

For Reflection

Do you care about your people?

How do you show it?

Can you identify something that is personally important to each member of the team you directly manage?

2

REALIZE: TO MOST PEOPLE, IT'S ONLY A JOB

You are renting a worker's behavior, not buying his or her soul. You have a right to expect professional and productive behavior on the job. Demand that, but stop when the end-of-the-day whistle blows.

In More Depth

Don't expect your employees to have the same dedication to work that you have. The reason you're the boss is because you see the work world from a different perspective. A few will aspire to join management ranks. Support them in this, but realize that they will be the exception.

The problem comes from the boss who expects people to work overtime (because he does); to take work home at night (because she does); to forgo family and personal interests (because he does); to have work be the center of their lives (because management does).

Managers and leaders should set an example, but realize the difference between setting an example and making a covert demand.

Most people want to enjoy work, be productive, be acknowledged personally and financially for their work, and then leave work and enjoy their family, friends, and activities. They do not want to mentally be "at work" 24 hours a day.

The consequences of ignoring this rule will be high turnover, covert or overt resentment, and potential sabotage of the work system.

The Idea in Action

Walt was a successful manager in an architectural firm, very driven and demanding. He had risen to managerial rank precisely because of this. He expected his professional and support staff to have the same level of commitment he did.

While office hours were 9 to 5, he expected people to come in early and frequently to work late (not just on special projects). If they didn't, their raises were less or they were subtly snubbed by him. He rescheduled planned employee vacations because of his perceived work demands. Even taking a full lunch break met with a frown.

Since he set the example—coming in earlier, working later, working through lunch, and so forth—Walt believed this was acceptable (and desirable). To get his message across, he delighted in telling the story of his first child's birth, when he rushed from work to take his wife to the hospital and was back at his desk within an hour after the birth.

Walt's only frustrations were: On average, employees stayed with the firm 19 months instead of the seven-plus years normal in his area. People were constantly complaining about not being paid for overtime. He was involved in several lawsuits filed by employees. And occasionally a project seemed mysteriously to go awry at a critical moment, even though his staff was thoroughly competent.

For Reflection

How would your employees describe your attitude about work and personal life?

How do you make the distinction between "setting an example" and making covert demands.

How do you balance your work life with your personal life?

3
HONOR DIFFERENCES

Every area has its own culture, customs, and minorities. Learn, respect, and value these differences. Incorporate them into your management.

In More Depth

The workplace is filled with a mixture of people: women, men, young, old, gay, straight, handicapped, veteran, and people of all ethnic backgrounds. Within each of these groups, there are different personalities, family backgrounds, life experiences, and the like.

Honor differences. Look for the common ground. Like a tapestry, all the different colors and designs add to the richness. Each color and element of design is different, its true beauty is in how it contributes to the whole.

Since we are not all the same, we each bring a unique gift to the workplace. Unfortunately, some managers also think we each bring a unique problem. It's like the old axiom: Is the glass half-full or half-empty? You see what you want to see.

Because of our uniqueness, we all see the world from our own special perspective. While this adds to the dialogue on how to do things, it can sometimes be difficult for managers who try to manage in just one way. You will need to learn to manage different people in different ways. What motivates one person may not motivate another.

Learn about the differences. Value and utilize the unique gifts. Ask questions. Try to understand. You won't always get it right, but you will come closer to perfection and you will learn a lot along the way.

The Idea in Action

At 57, Aaron had been with his company for 19 years, the past 6 in a managerial slot. He was a Korean War veteran, lived in a prosperous suburb, and came from a midwestern, middle-class family background.

He managed the marketing department of a holding company for a large chain of gas stations, based in Denver. He was asked and agreed to move to Los Angeles to oversee marketing for the western region.

When he met his new staff, Aaron discovered there were more minorities than there had been on his staff in Denver. Certainly diversity was not new to him, but this was unexpected. In fact, he was the minority. The thought of dealing with so many cultural, ethnic, and lifestyle differences made him tense.

But Aaron was fair and open-minded. He faced up to his biases, albeit with some anxiety, but also with a commitment to make this work. He asked questions, learned about the people and their backgrounds, and tried hard to accommodate the differences while focusing on producing results for the company. Sometimes it was awkward; always it was enlightening; and it earned him the respect of his staff.

For Reflection

In the unit where you work, how many different religious, ethnic, lifestyle, and other kinds of differences can you identify?

If you listed these different categories, could you write down three unique aspects of each group that help the workplace?

What biases and prejudices do you have? Which would you be willing to modify if it would make the workplace more pleasant and productive?

4

SAY THANK YOU

Express your gratitude for a job well done, and mean it. People produce extraordinary results when they feel appreciated.

In More Depth

We all like to feel that someone appreciates us and the work we do. It's not uncommon to walk through offices and see people displaying a thank-you card from the boss, a special note from a customer, or an award (which may be years old). Praise works!

Thank your team members. Compliment them on their successes and accomplishments. Tell them when they've made progress. You can do this one-on-one, publicly, in verbal or written form, or any number of creative ways. When people are shown appreciation for doing something, they are much more likely to do more of it.

Showing appreciation sends a message about what you want and what you consider valuable. Without that kind of feedback, your people may make wrong assumptions about what is acceptable or valued.

Research shows that people are hungry for recognition. When they receive genuine praise for something well done, not only will they feel internally rewarded, but they will also gain stature among family and friends. This, in turn, increases their regard for you as leader. The cycle becomes self-sustaining. Once a praiseworthy level of performance is seen to be possible, people will act and work to live up to the impression they've made.

The Idea in Action

Terri M. was the manager of a mayoral campaign for a leading candidate. She was a real leader, inspiring staff and volunteers alike. Her motivational speeches were phenomenal, producing tears, laughter, and cheers. As campaign manager, she was extremely busy running from one appointment to the next, showing up at headquarters or rallies just in time.

Over time, Terri noticed a disturbing pattern. Right after one of her speeches or whenever she was present, productivity skyrocketed, but the longer she was away, the more productivity declined. It was as if they needed her presence to perform.

Fortunately, one of the volunteers was a talented professional personnel manager. This person told Terri that her people needed more than a speech to keep them motivated over the long run. They needed to know what was expected of them, what was a valued activity, and they needed to be recognized for performing that activity.

Though it was against her nature, Terri decided to cut back on the motivational speeches to staff and devote that time to praising them for specific successes and accomplishments. It worked! There wasn't as much electricity in the air, but people were happy and motivated. They knew what was expected and what was prized behavior. They were hungry for the recognition, especially from such a charismatic leader.

Terri learned that the praise and thanks not only heightened motivation but also produced the same positive behaviors over and over.

For Reflection

When was the last time you thanked someone on your staff?
When was the last time you sincerely praised someone for doing an outstanding job?
What have you noticed today that should be praised?

5

ASK YOUR EMPLOYEES WHAT THEY NEED

Find out what your employees need from you in order to get the job done.

In More Depth

One of the best ways to be effective is to ensure the effectiveness of your employees. Conversely, if your people are not working at close to capacity, you're not either. Don't automatically assume it's going to cost a lot of money. It's often minor things that stop employees from doing a job done most efficiently.

No one knows better how to make a job more efficient than the person doing that job. Ask your people what they need. Here are some of the answers you'll frequently hear: simple office supplies, quicker access to information, quicker responses to questions addressed to management, time or help in taking care of routine stuff so it doesn't pile up, flextime to accommodate a special need, or feedback on work being done.

Sometimes it's more complicated. A purchasing department may need more latitude in dealing with special suppliers, or a secretary may need access to files normally secured by management. In cases like these, spend some time to determine whether the potential improvement justifies the expense and time called for.

The key is to ask, because they're not likely to volunteer the information. Following this rule offers a low-cost way to dramatically improve productivity.

The Idea in Action

Dr. Johnson was dean of the business school at a small liberal arts college in the Northwest. The school operated fairly successfully, but he suspected that many of the people were not operating at full capacity.

He decided to begin a program of asking one person per day what he or she needed to do the job better. He resolved to keep at it until he had asked every person, from the lowest paid to the most prestigious. To show he meant business, he committed to respond to each request in one of three ways: "Yes, and here's when..."; "No, and here's why..."; or "This needs some research. I'll get back to you with an answer by such and such a time."

When word spread of what he was doing, productivity increased simply owing to the attention and respect he was showing the staff by going through this process. Some of the many changes were: allowing secretaries to answer questions on routine nonacademic matters which previously had been handled by professors; freeing professors from some administrative tasks and allowing them to devote more time to counseling students; giving teaching assistants a small budget for materials instead of relying on their mentor professor's budget.

The results far exceeded Dr. Johnson's most optimistic expectations, and the overall cost was quite low considering the time savings and other benefits.

For Reflection

When was the last time you asked your staff what they needed to get their job done better?

What are some of your success stories about increasing productivity by getting people what they needed?

What do you need to do your job better?

6

LOYALTY BEGETS LOYALTY

Loyalty is the natural response to loyalty. For the most part, you get back what you put out.

In More Depth

People usually respond in the same manner that they are treated: respect commands respect; arrogance returns arrogance; loyalty builds loyalty.

Loyalty means looking after someone's best interest and sticking with him or her in bad times and good. It means a commitment for the long term. It means focusing on the good in the relationship and minimizing the trouble when things get rocky. It does not mean placating people, ignoring problems, or sacrificing yourself or the company. Nor does it mean you owe someone a job, especially if he or she is not performing.

The manager-managee relationship is like a marriage. It is a commitment that demonstrates itself over the years, not just during the honeymoon. You develop mutually satisfying goals. You enjoy the comfort and security that comes from really knowing and liking people, despite their inadequacies. You do things for each other because you care, not because you have to.

The Idea in Action

Elizabeth B. was a senior partner of a regional accounting firm. She had been a clerk for the firm during college, and was hired as a junior auditor after graduation. Her career continued to grow over the next 17 years until she was made a partner.

When she was progressing through the ranks, the senior ranking partner had a reputation for being loyal to his employees. When business was slow, he would go out and personally try to drum up extra business to avoid having to lay people off. When people had personal problems, he still demanded productivity, but was flexible on the pace of their improvement; and he supported his people when a client complained—as long as they were defensible. He didn't cut someone down just to appease a client.

The most memorable demonstration of loyalty Elizabeth experienced with him was when she made a mistake that cost the firm thousands of dollars. He could have fired her, but he told her she was valuable to the firm and he was more interested in their long-term professional relationship.

Elizabeth received several very good job offers from competitors over the years. Any one of them would have offered more money. One even offered a partnership earlier than her current firm. But she stayed loyal to her boss and the firm because she valued the loyalty shown to her. There was safety, security, and integrity in their demonstration of commitment.

Over the years she has made the firm a great deal of money, and her hard-earned expertise and intimate knowledge of clients' situations are highly prized. Is it any wonder this firm has low turnover and high morale?

For Reflection

Would your employees say you were loyal to them?
How do you demonstrate your loyalty to your employees?
Do you think loyalty is worth the extra effort and additional cost involved?

7

ADMIT WHEN YOU ARE WRONG...AND QUICKLY

By owning up to your mistakes, you clear the air and send an important message about responsibility.

In More Depth

If you're making so many mistakes that you can't admit to a few, then the problem is not in the admissions. We all make mistakes, so why are people so unwilling to admit an error?

When you make a mistake, admit it. It's important to do this at the time you realize it, while it is affecting people. Otherwise, it looks like you're trying to shift the blame. Tell the involved party or parties what, if anything, you can and will do to correct it. If the damage is irreversible, an apology is the only recourse, so apologize.

Mistakes seldom go unnoticed. Besides, most of the energy spent trying to cover up just prolongs the misery and increases the pressure by taking time and attention away from the solution. When you do admit your errors, people develop respect for your integrity, honesty, and humanity. And they will be more likely to trust you in other matters.

The Idea in Action

Although she started as a clerk, Julie F. quickly demonstrated an ability to manage, and was now manager of the jewelry department in a major department store. During the holiday season the store needed extra sales help, so they hired a number of college students who needed the income.

Julie liked these students but felt a bit envious that they were working toward college degrees, whereas she had decided to work instead of attending college. It made her very sensitive to her status as boss. She wanted to prove herself to them.

During a particularly busy week, as she made out the schedule for the following week, she inadvertently failed to schedule two students and overscheduled two others who didn't want so many hours. When she handed out the schedule, they looked at her quizzically but said nothing. When she went back and reviewed it, she discovered the oversight.

It really was an insignificant thing that could easily be corrected, but whatever the reason, Julie couldn't bring herself to admit having made an error. She even went so far as to insist that she had planned it that way, making up reasons why the two had been left off and the other two were expected to do more. This only aggravated matters, and they asked her to reconsider. She refused, saying it was a matter of principle, but she was keenly aware of the glares and whispering for the rest of the day. In her heart she knew this was only going to get worse.

That night, she decided to bite the bullet, admit she had made a mistake, and then had compounded it by trying to cover up. She feared they would laugh at her and think she was stupid. So she was surprised the next day to hear them say they appreciated the forthrightness with which she handled the situation. It was she who had been making things more uncomfortable than they had to be.

For Reflection

How do you react when you realize you've made a mistake?
What have been your experiences after admitting a mistake, bad or good?
How long does it take you to get around to admitting a mistake?

8

AUTHORITY MUST EQUAL RESPONSIBILITY

If authority doesn't equal responsibility, it's a setup for an employee to fail. That's not fair.

In More Depth

Making people responsible for a task without giving them the corresponding authority to cause it to happen virtually assures their failure.

Consider this scenario: "Pat, see that this project gets done by June 15. I can't spare any people to help you. Our budget won't allow any extra expenditure. Use your creativity, but don't upset anyone. And if you figure out a way to get more people or money, I can't back you up."

Ridiculous, right? It happens every day in the world of business. Managers give an assignment and hold a person responsible, but for a million and one "reasons" hold back the authority to get it done. Perhaps they feel they're giving away their power.

Consequently, it destroys morale. People in Pat's shoes feel they're being set up as scapegoats in case things fail. And they may be right. Even the positive thinkers figure it'll only be luck if they pull it off.

The Idea in Action

Lois was manager of a city housing department. Though knowledgeable and experienced, over the years she had come to sense that her staff had developed some animosity toward her. She was a nice person and acted with integrity, so she couldn't understand this.

One day a senior supervisor was retiring. Knowing he had nothing to fear now, Lois asked him directly what he thought was going on. He was not shy in telling her one of his major problems with her style.

"We respect your technical competence and your concern, but by your actions, you send a signal that you don't trust us. Many of us feel you have set us up to fail over the years."

Lois was shocked and asked for an example. He responded without hesitation, "I'll never forget the time you told us there were to be no more delays in getting the product to market. When we protested that the production department was understaffed and couldn't handle the volume, you told us to `use our influence.' Then you insinuated very strongly that if it didn't happen, we `wouldn't all be here this time next year.' It didn't, of course, because we didn't control the resources to make anything happen differently. And after all, you didn't fire anyone. A couple quit, but nothing else changed."

Lois was disturbed by his comments. For the first time she saw herself through the eyes of those she managed. Thereafter, she tried to be more sensitive to this complaint, and she began to see how she herself was sometimes put in the same situation. Did this kind of thing go all the way to the top of the organization, she wondered.

For Reflection

When you hold people responsible for something, do you give them the authority to accomplish it?

How would you describe your management philosophy about balancing responsibility and authority?

Have you personally ever felt like you were responsible for something but did not really have the authority to do it? How did it feel?

Company Politics

9

MANAGEMENT IS AN ARTIFICIAL ROLE

Unlike a family role or a friendship, the management role is not natural. You won't always be liked or popular, and frequently it is not fun.

In More Depth

Your relationship to people, when you are the manager, and they are your employees, is an artificial one. With friends and family, you want to be together and you choose to be together. In the management relationship, you are thrown together and not everyone likes it. It often means making decisions people will disagree with.

Some managers try to make their relationship with their employees into a social one. While that is neither inherently good or bad, it can complicate the operation. Social relationships with employees only work when kept totally separate, without bearing on the main focus. If you ever have to question a good business decision because it might harm a personal relationship with an employee, then you have crossed the line.

You have the managerial role because you were chosen to get results, not because you won a popularity contest. The relationship is based on logic, not on emotion. Anything more is a bonus.

The Idea in Action

Deborah R. was manager of admissions and records for a state college. She received the promotion to manager because she knew her job well and had good people skills.

When she was first in the managerial position, she wanted to be liked. Having "come from the ranks" she was friends with many of the other employees, and didn't want them to think the job had gone to her head.

She soon found herself being lobbied by certain employees to do things their way. It became difficult to make certain assignments, especially when there was to be a reduction in force. She also heard rumors that some of her staff felt her old friends were being favored for the best assignments.

Deborah valued her friendships with these people, but she felt they were compromising her effectiveness and her freedom to make decisions. She decided to have a meeting with all her staff and lay everything on the table. "Being a manager requires a certain detachment from my personal relationships," she said. "I value the friendships I have with many of you, but treating everyone equally must take precedence. Friendship can never be a basis for any of my decisions. So I'm asking that friendship not be used as an avenue to lobby me on decisions. I am also asking for your understanding and support when I must make a decision with which you might disagree."

This freed Deborah to act as a manager and interact authentically with her staff. Ironically, it probably preserved several friendships which, had her dilemma continued, could have been damaged.

For Reflection

How often do you have to question how someone with whom you have a personal relationship will react to a business decision?

Are you, and your employees, clear about your working and personal relationships at the office?

How have you felt and reacted earlier in your career when a boss abdicated the managerial role in favor of a social role?

10

DON'T HITCH YOUR WAGON TO ANYONE ELSE'S STAR

Every organization has its fast risers who appear to have bright futures. But stars sometimes burn out. If you are attached, you may fall too. Be your own star.

In More Depth

One of the most common career traps is attaching yourself to someone else's star, otherwise known as riding their coattails. This is a hard one. It seems to make so much sense, and it feels so right to take advantage of being associated with someone who is rising rapidly or has great influence. While there are short-term payoffs (and, admittedly, some long-term ones), it's a dangerous game.

Stars have a way of burning out, or being burned out, or facing a crowd who is out to burn them out. Business books are full of stories of people who rise to the top and then fizzle. Think how many officers of giant companies have "taken retirement" in just the past six months.

When you're hooked to someone else's star, you get a free ride, but you don't control the ride. Better to concentrate on being your own star. The shining light that comes from inside you can't be extinguished.

The Idea in Action

Ray was a bright, well-educated assistant to the divisional manager of a major insurance firm. Though his boss liked his work and said he was destined to move up the ladder, Ray wanted to rise rapidly.

He noticed that Tim W. was the very successful manager for another division and requested a transfer to work on a project for him—not a problem in itself, but Ray did it for the association, not the experience.

It worked. Tim received another promotion and asked Ray to join him on a new project. The cycle played out yet again, with another promotion for each of them. Along the way, Tim was making enemies. He bulldozed his way through, ignoring people's feelings. He got results, but established no loyalties.

Eventually he had made enough enemies that, while there was no overt mutiny, there was enough resistance to make his job difficult and the results next to impossible to achieve. His star faded. He became angry. It ultimately led to his dismissal.

Ray now faced a dilemma. Though not fired, he was aware that he had not built any support in the organization and was known only as Tim's protege. Realizing his mistake, he vowed not to repeat it. He left of his own will and joined another company. This time, Ray focused on his own work and rose more slowly but more surely. At last report, he was VP at a finance company and still rising.

For Reflection

Whom do you know in your organization who is tying himself or herself to someone else's star?

Are you known for you own work, or as someone else's right hand?

How would you counsel someone who was tempted to tie himself or herself to someone else instead of developing his or her own reputation?

11

CHOOSE YOUR WORDS CAREFULLY

Realize that your words may carry more weight than you think, and that there is a difference between what you say and what is heard.

In More Depth

Authority and position give your words extra clout. You know you're the same person the kids feel free to argue with, that you don't always have the answers, that sometimes you just think out loud, like most people. You don't see yourself as different, but you are.

When you take on the mantle of management, your words change in the ears and minds of employees. What may seem like a casual discussion to you often seems like a life and death dialogue to employees. They go home at night and tell their partners and families what an incredible, brilliant, awful, or rude thing you said.

You may have just been testing the waters. An employees often mistake such explorations as official decrees. If you casually remark, "It would be nice to have a new cafeteria," you can be sure that, word will spread that the boss said we're getting a new cafeteria.

As an exercise that will give you a sense of this, multiply the intensity of your words fivefold, and then mentally listen to your conversation again.

The Idea in Action

As community editor at a large newspaper, Margarita had 17 reporters and 39 staff people working under her. She was active in church and in raising her two children, and saw herself as a working mother who happened to have a good job.

Her employees, however, saw her as an effective, sometimes tough leader, always focused on deadlines, producing quality work, and creating innovative stories. They also saw her as a trailblazer because she was the first woman at the newspaper to enter the executive ranks.

Margarita viewed the casual meetings and lunch breaks in the cafeteria as friendly discussions with colleagues. She often felt relaxed enough to talk off the top of her head. Her staff, on the other hand, believed every word was carefully calculated and even discussed it throughout the rest of the day, "What do you think she meant by that?"

Finally, Margarita realized her words were carrying far more weight than she intended. She had to do what the employees already thought she was doing, carefully consider all nuances of her conversations. When she wanted to brainstorm, she had to make it very clear that she was just exploring, so no one would assume she was making policy.

She mourned the loss of that freedom of expression, but she gained a sense of excitement about the possibility that she could influence the organization subtly through her language.

For Reflection

How do your employees and colleagues differentiate when you are just brainstorming and when you are making policy announcements? Be honest, how can they really tell?

Think back to a recent conversation and consider how an employee may have heard it differently than you meant it.

Are you willing to put some rigor into the way you communicate with your colleagues and staff?

12

KNOW YOUR OBLIGATIONS

When opinions clash, know whose interests you represent, and whose goals you are being paid to meet or fulfill.

In More Depth

We all face competing demands for our time, efforts, and allegiances. Your employees may want you to do one thing, your boss another. What do you do? Both can make life difficult. Most likely, barring a compelling reason to the contrary, you would respond to your boss. But you should explain to each side the interests and views of the other.

It's trickier if the competing desires are between your boss and someone higher up. Though you shouldn't have to take sides, such sometimes you must. In this case, you should work things out with your immediate boss. It's his or her job to do the same up the ladder. Again, though, a memo explaining your position is nice insurance.

Finally, consider these guiding thoughts:

· It depends on how important the matter is. Sometimes you can get away with a decision your boss disagrees with. Sometimes not.

· Consider what's best for the organization, but don't act without discussing it up and down the ladder.

. In organization run by consensus, listen, have an opinion, voice it, but remember who pays your salary and controls your future.

Do this thinking before trouble arises, because it inevitably will.

The Idea in Action

As manager of a small chain of newspapers on the East Coast, Carol S. had to make a decision about assigning several large accounts which had virtually fallen in her lap. Her sales staff wanted it done according to seniority in the firm. Her boss thought it should be done on the basis of which people had the best success rate. Carol herself preferred to assign people according to which account required the most creative touch, regardless of seniority or dollars.

Carol had to ask herself, "Where do my responsibilities lie? To whom am I most responsible?" This was a major decision, so she couldn't ignore her boss's view, even though she disagreed. Finally, she just wrote up all the possible options, including the decision she would make if on her own, and sent it to her boss. The boss then pointed out something she hadn't thought of: that although new, two of the accounts were subsidiaries of major existing accounts. One company was run by the brother of her company's CEO. It was not a time for either experimentation or status quo.

Actually, Carol could accept this, and when she passed it on to her people, they saw the logic too. The real lessons were two: that each case has to be dealt with separately, and that the boss usually is in better touch with what's best for the organization.

For Reflection

Who sets the goals that you are obligated to achieve?

Who are the various constituencies that may lobby for your loyalty, e.g., employees, boss, board.

How would you address each of them if their interests conflicted?

13

TAKE TIME TO READ THE ENVIRONMENT

When entering a leadership position, listen, observe, and stand back at first. Early appearances can be deceptive. Until you know the organization and its people, do not form alliances.

In More Depth

When you're new to a job, you don't know the history and culture of the organization, so don't rush to ally with any particular person or group. That goes for people both higher and lower in the organization.

Your fresh perspective frees you to make assessments unhindered by old ways of doing things. Avoid being seduced by these early impressions. Hold your fire until you've checked them out.

When you come aboard, there certainly will be some good, important people who will be trying to impress you, and you will want to recognize them. There will also be unproductive people who can make great first impressions. They can be dangerous.

It is a little more delicate when a higher ranking manager wants you in his camp. Obviously, you want to develop good relationships among upper management. However, some are vicious, some are simply incompetent, and some have been put out to pasture. It's possible to be friendly and supportive without letting your reputation get linked with people who are less than quality material.

Everyone wants something from you. That's how business works. Just take your time and don't spend your "honeymoon period" capital too early.

The Idea in Action

Kwame was the new training manager for a chain of grocery stores. He had come from a competing company and had a fine reputation within the industry. He succeeded a weak training manager who had left "under duress."

During the first several days on the job, most of his staff welcomed him. Several asked him out for lunch. He was invited to the secretaries' monthly happy hour at the local watering hole. He was also greeted by other managers within the company, two of whom wanted private conferences to "let him know what's going on."

Reluctant to give the appearance of favoritism, Kwame hedged on the luncheon engagements until later, saying that he was going to just run to the deli until he got his office in order.

Ninety percent of the information Kwame would have received would have been useful. The people offering it generally had the organization's best interests at heart. Ten percent could lead Kwame down a very dangerous path, because at least one of the people seeking his attention was already targeted for firing. Kwame knew all this instinctively. But how can one tell the useful majority from the dangerous few?

The fact is, you can't—at least not at first. By holding off on making alliances, Kwame increased his odds of deciding wisely in the long run.

For Reflection

Can you discipline yourself enough to hold out until you're sure where you should form alliances?

Have you had any negative experiences because you were too quick to get involved with a person or issue?

How much can you trust your intuition in new situations? From past history, how many of your first impressions were valid?

14
CONTACTS ARE GOLD

Build alliances. Get to know people. At some point you will need people's help to get things done.

In More Depth

You've heard the old saying, "It's not what you know; it's whom you know." Actually, you need both. To get things done requires more than technique and skill. You need the knowledge, insights, and support of other people. If you want to move up, cultivate contacts from a variety of constituencies, not just within your own company, but industrywide, and even in other areas not directly related.

There is more to mining contacts than having their names in your Rolodex. You should be in theirs as well. This shouldn't be done in a manipulative, self-serving manner. It has to be reciprocal. You must have something to offer, or some way to be of service to them.

You can become very valuable in your organization, and within your realm of influence, by developing a broad-based network of contacts. It gives you greater insight into your work and the environment in which you operate. Plus, it makes work more fun.

The Idea in Action

Larry Rose managed sales for a car dealership. He had heard all the put-downs about car sales people and was determined to overcome the bad image. If a customer wanted something other than what he had to offer, he referred the person to another dealership. He made recommendations about service stations, insurance agents, car wash places, specialty auto supply houses, and noticed that customers viewed him as a valuable resource when he did. Even if it did not produce an immediate sale or income to him, he found that customers appreciated these referrals, and often rewarded his helpfulness by referring business to him.

Larry decided to make a game of it and "roll out" the concept. Because he was involved in several civic organizations, was active in church, and met many different people each day, he began asking people what they did, got their cards, and began referring all sorts of people for everything imaginable. He'd link people up to CPAs, cooks, lawyers, carpenters, fund-raising experts, journalists. There really was no limit. Pretty soon, "Ask Larry; he knows everybody" was the common answer to anyone who wanted to know whom to call about anything.

Since he was doing it to be helpful, and not just to get business for himself, you can imagine the good will and economic benefit generated among all involved. Larry's biggest reward, though, came one day as he was telling an advertising executive (who was buying a car) about his network of contacts. The guy said this kind of thing was a required skill in the advertising business, but he was surprised and impressed to see it applied with such savvy at an auto dealership—the image boost Larry had been seeking all along for people in his field.

For Reflection

How many contacts have you added to your list in the past month?

How have you helped or added value to people who are in your Rolodex?

Are you known as a resource of contacts within your company, industry or community? Could you become that?

15
DON'T BURN YOUR BRIDGES

Conduct yourself with integrity and grace. You never know what past actions can come back to haunt you.

In More Depth

Be very careful about burning your bridges. Granted, there are times when you are leaving a job that has been a bad experience, and you want to tell people how awful the others were or what a terrible place it was.

But is the momentary pleasure of telling someone off worth the long-term damage it can cause? What happens when you need a good reference? If you think the law protects you from being bad-mouthed, think again. There are very subtle ways you can be undercut. Reputations and stories spread. Most organizational leaders belong to the same groups, meet in their churches, and talk at community events. If you're high enough on the ladder, any good boss will check you out in the informal network. Forget about trying to control this.

You may also need to develop contacts within your old company again, especially if it is in the same field or is a competitor. What happens if it acquires or merges with your new company? What happens if you want to get involved in a prestigious organization, perhaps a country club, and people from the old place are on the board? What happens if you start your own business and find you need your old contacts to make it successful? Think about it.

The Idea in Action

Paula D. was a management consultant for a firm specializing in retailing operations. She and one of the principals of the firm didn't get along. Finally she had had enough and decided to leave.

The morning of her final day, she stormed into the principal's office and gave him a piece of her mind. She told him how awful he was, what a lousy job he did in running the firm and how she was going to advise everybody not to do business with ABC. Then she left and took a position with a competitor, XYZ Group.

With clients, Paula would make disparaging remarks about ABC. She noticed that the clients seemed uncomfortable with this, but she thought it helped get business. She also spoke negatively about ABC in other situations, like training seminars. After two years, XYZ was having trouble. Several large clients went with other firms, including ABC. There were layoffs, and Paula was among them. She had to find a new job.

Since people in consulting all belong to the same professional organizations, Paula's reputation kept her from getting hired. She decided to open her own firm, and found she had to compete against ABC for jobs. She noticed that whenever they were in competition, ABC would put all its resources behind the bid in order to get the contract, even to the point of undercutting all reasonable pricing. In short, by burning her bridges, Paula had made her life a lot more difficult.

For Reflection

Are you toying with the idea of telling someone off?

If you have "burned a bridge," can you repair it, and are you willing to do so?

How would you react (both short-term and long-term) to someone who told you off and bad-mouthed you and your organization to others?

Leadership

16

YOU ARE RESPONSIBLE FOR YOUR FEELINGS AND ACTIONS

We ultimately control our attitudes, feelings, and viewpoints. Employees reflect the attitude of the leader. Look to see if what you think and do are helping your organization succeed, or preventing it from succeeding.

In More Depth

Managers are human, too. They have emotions, likes and dislikes, and ways they view other people, situations, and the world in general. When you, as manager, walk into the workplace, you set the tone for the entire organization. If you're aggressive and angry, the company will be, too. If you're prejudiced, the organization will exhibit prejudice. If you're happy, the organization will reflect happiness.

It's impossible to eliminate all emotion and bias from your work life. You can, however, control your negative actions. The key is seeing which actions are harmful to the organization...or to yourself. For example, if you're grieving over a loss, it's okay to tell people so they can offer support, but don't let a negative tone jeopardize the corporate well-being.

On the positive side, if you're proud of the company, product, or people, let them know it. If you value employee involvement, set employees free to do what they have to do. Don't let personal issues get in the way of a positive presence or what's best for your group.

The Idea in Action

Pat was a salesperson with very definite views. She often professed a preference for "street smart" people over "highbrow MBAs." She felt the secret of success was pure hard work, and teased people who let their feelings get in the way of a sale. She herself could be moody, sometimes joyous, sometimes down, but she was careful not to let customers see her emotional side. And because she toughed it out when she felt depressed, she was very successful.

As sometimes occurs, Pat was promoted to management, because of her sales prowess, not her managerial ability. Subsequently, at sales meetings she would often interject her biases: "Don't waste your time calling on anyone lower than president," she would say. Too often, emotions that she would have concealed from customers were allowed to surface among peers and reports, and she would wonder why everyone was so "down" that day.

Predictably, her sales team began to lose momentum. The VP called her in and pointed out the effect she was having on people around her. It was suggested that she see these people as customers, too, people who needed what she was selling—in this case, a positive attitude. After all, she always set a great tone for outside customers. She tried it, conducting meetings more professionally, keeping her ego in check. She learned to deal with MBA types. Instead of insisting on "just one more call," she acted more sympathetically when one of her team was having a problem.

The result: Sales took off again. Her career was salvaged.

For Reflection

What's the point of this story?

Do you have biases or prejudices that show up in the workplace?

If you asked your peers or employees for honest feedback, how would they describe the "tone" you set for the organization?

17

DON'T PUT YOURSELF ON A PEDESTAL

The world no longer recognizes the divine right of kings. Being manager requires more responsibility, not less. Avoid double standards.

In More Depth

We know that employees mirror the attitudes and integrity of their leaders. This rule goes a step further. The higher you go, the more integrity and leadership you must show.

Being boss requires leadership in deed as well as word. Managers cannot afford to operate above the rules they themselves set. If you demand that everyone do something a certain way, don't do it differently yourself. If there is a compelling reason for an exception, then explain the logic or change the rule. If subordinates are expected always to be open and truthful to you, you must do the same. If something is confidential, either say nothing or say candidly that you can't speak to that issue. If you expect a full day's work from them, put in a full day (or longer) yourself. If you expect them to work together as a team, don't put them at cross purposes with each other.

People hate hypocrisy. They're quick to spot it and unsympathetic in putting it down.

The Idea in Action

Evan was promoted to be manager of a large furniture store. He had worked hard for this and loved the idea of having people work for him and of being more visible. Having chafed under old Mr. Tanner for years, he was determined to do things differently and enjoy the position.

At first, Evan came in punctually at 9:00 a.m., but that soon slipped to 9:30, and occasionally even 10:00. After all, he was the boss. He could do what he wanted. Besides, he reasoned, he did work late sometimes. But he was ruthless with other people about their arrival times and wondered why there seemed to be so much resistance to his demands.

He made a point of telling employees that their suggestions were important to him, but he seldom adopted any and never explained why. Ideas just seemed to die. He wondered why he got fewer and fewer suggestions as time went on. He stretched his expenses when he was traveling. After all, he thought, it's a management perk. Perhaps because he knew the tricks, he caught every extra mile deduction his outside sales associate submitted. Now he wondered why his bookkeeper no longer confided in him when she suspected cheating on an expense report.

He felt that certain information was inappropriate for employees to know. If challenged, he would just try to snow the person or stretch the truth. When asked to do something, he was quick to say yes. So what if it took longer than expected or got moved to a lower priority. He didn't have to explain. He was the boss.

Although they never said anything, ultimately, Evan began to feel none of his people trusted him. He found himself losing trust in them, and he wondered why.

For Reflection

Do you live up to the rules you enforce?
What does integrity mean to you?
Do you set higher standards of integrity for yourself or your employees?

18

STUDY IS NOT A SUBSTITUTE FOR TIMELY DECISION MAKING

The ability to make decisions is what separates leaders from followers.

In More Depth

Organizations move forward only as a result of decisions being made. And it is the manager's job to move the organization forward. There will be times when you will be tempted to stall a decision until more information is available. Sometimes that's appropriate. More often, though, it's not. Information doesn't make decisions, you do!

Research, study, and due consideration are very important. It would be foolish to try to run a business without gathering information. But seldom will you have all the information you would like on an issue. So, you simply assess what you do have, make your best decision, and deal with the consequences.

Decision making requires developing trust in yourself and your ability. It's also important to realize that you may not always make the "right" decision. The goal, however, is to make good decisions. If you never make a wrong decision, you're not taking enough risks.

It is natural for someone new to a situation to experience fear when making decisions. In that case, it helps to remember that in most cases, you will have subsequent chances to put things back on course.

The leader who makes a mistake but continues to make lots of good decisions—rather than "deciding not to decide"—will be successful.

The Idea in Action

Kelly had worked his way up the ranks and had been promoted to the corporate ranks. He was now managing about five times as many people as before and a budget about six times greater. His new position was highly visible.

To start, Kelly set up a strategic plan for his unit. The plan was well prepared, with adequate information. It was reviewed by senior management and accepted. Things went well and business accelerated. The plan soon became outdated as Kelly's unit exceeded expectations. Many points needed reconsideration to sustain the momentum. He had some information he felt was valid, but he wanted more. He was beginning to fall into the "perfect decision" trap.

The fast pace of events put Kelly in a dilemma. He could not afford to deliberate long over decisions, but he felt that if he made a mistake, it would ruin him. Fear set in. Finally, realizing that further delay was as dangerous as making the wrong decision, Kelly took the plunge on the basis of the data he had.

Over the next six months, a few of his decisions fizzled, but he made follow-up decisions to correct the mistakes. And overall, enough worked out well to carry him over the fear barrier. He was on his way to another promotion.

For Reflection

What decisions have you been putting off which really should be made?

When you make a decision, should you be gathering more information or making the decision faster with less information?

What do you imagine will happen if you do make a mistake by making a decision? How likely is that to really happen?

19

BE VISIBLE

Leading means being out front. Create "presence" in the workplace. People want to see you.

In More Depth

Sending a memo telling someone to do something is not leadership. Your people need to see you. Don't hide away in your office or get so involved with outside activities that you seldom spend time with them. To lead, you must provide direction. To do that, you must be seen and heard.

Many managers fall into traps that take them away from their people. Some like status too much and believe only projects outside their own work environment are worthy of their attention. Others get bored and concentrate on things that interest them more than everyday operations. Some actually fear interaction with their employees. Many executives have had to return to the trenches after realizing that their absence allowed the operation to deteriorate. At that point, being there isn't much fun.

Just seeing the boss creates an atmosphere of stability, collegiality, and teamwork. If they don't see or hear from you, your people will create their own sense of team—without you—and go in their own direction, which may not be the direction you want.

The Idea in Action

Katie was head of the community food bank in a major metropolitan area that had become a model for other food banks across the country.

In the last two years, she had tired of meeting with staff and volunteers to give them the "rah rah talk," as she called it. In earlier years, she had referred to it as "meeting with my partners to fulfill our mission."

She was being invited to speak to other food banks across the country to impart her wisdom, experience, and motivation. She was good at these appearances and at being an expert motivator. She was so good and enjoyed it so much that she was out of town about nine days per month. When she was in town, she met with other community leaders on civic projects and sat on the boards of several charities.

At the office, she spent most of her time at meetings with brass, and seldom "walked the house," as she referred to her tour of the warehouse.

Over the year, fewer volunteers had come forward, and morale slipped. Donations declined, and people were saying it wasn't fun anymore. They wondered if the pressure of being the model wasn't too much, and if it was for real, anyhow, since things didn't seem that wonderful anymore.

Katie called a professional contact she hadn't seen in some time. He had just to disappeared from the speaking/luncheon circuit. He told her he had lost touch and needed to give more attention and commitment to his primary operation and his people, and to renew his leadership. Divine message, Katie thought as she said good-bye. Change starts tomorrow.

For Reflection

How often do your employees see and hear you?

How many of your employees can you call by name?

On a 1-to-10 scale, how well do you think your employees know your vision for the operation; your plans for their future; your commitment to their and the operation's success; know you?

20

DEAL WITH IT OR LIVE WITH IT

Deal with issues as they arise. That which you avoid gets bigger and bigger. Delaying makes you look afraid and ineffective.

In More Depth

Every manager is tempted to ignore a problem or an issue at one time or another, but dealing with problems expeditiously is critical. This doesn't mean reacting without thinking. It's just a matter of keeping the environment clear of lingering distractions.

The kinds of problems managers most often avoid are the tough personnel issues: problem employees, morale, minority sensitivity, sexual harassment, or even an employee who has body odor. It's also tempting to ignore market-share erosion, deterioration of plant and equipment, and problems with your product or service. If you don't deal with these things, they will grow at the expense of your respect, and remain nagging distractions until you take the necessary action to resolve them.

Sometimes problems do seem to go away with time (albeit rarely). This doesn't relieve you of the responsibility to respond. Your employees and stakeholders are looking to you for leadership. They have a right to expect a considered response. If you avoid it, you will be seen as weak and ineffective in handling tough situations.

The Idea in Action

Peggy Fencil was the accounts payable supervisor in a large retail store.

She had a strong need to be liked, and treated her employees like family. Initially, Peggy's promotion was greeted with great excitement. She followed an unpopular "hardball" supervisor. Her staff was delighted with her mothering.

A year into the job, operations were still going well, but Peggy felt her staff wasn't as responsive as they had been at first. Over the next year she felt morale decline even more. She wanted to do a good job, so she took her lead clerk, someone she trusted to speak the truth, into her confidence.

After Peggy assured her confidentiality, the clerk responded, "You're too nice. Betty comes in late. You talk to her. She still comes in late. John talks too much. He quiets down when you mention it, but he's back at it in a couple of weeks. Everyone has to cover for Lulu because she's so slow, but she always gets acceptable evaluations. The group figures that if others are allowed to get by with murder, why go out of their way?"

Peggy was shocked. She had done her best to create a happy working atmosphere. After a sleepless night and some checking the next day, she determined that her confidante was right.

She tackled the problems the following Monday. There were some unhappy moments, especially with the specific employees involved, but they knew they had been living on borrowed time, so they began to come around. Peggy was more amazed than anyone to see how fast morale turned around. Better yet, having dealt with the problems, she could now devote her attention to more creative endeavors.

For Reflection

What are the three most important problems or issues you've been avoiding?
How would you describe your willingness to deal with tough issues?
What would your staff say about your willingness to deal with problems?

21

STAY THE COURSE

Once your goal and direction have been set, don't stray unless absolutely necessary. Consistency is often better than constantly changing in search of the perfect route.

In More Depth

There is more than a grain of truth in the old saying, "Providence moves when someone becomes committed."

There is a special satisfaction in setting your sights on a goal and then focusing all your energy until you reach it. Knowing how to change is good, but people and organizations need stability, too, and that must come from the manager. An organization's leaders must decide at some point what course to take for a task, project, or entire operation. Once decided, it's your job to hold the course and concentrate your resources on maintaining it.

Obviously, if you find yourself going the wrong way, you need to adjust. Do not, however, change with every new possibility or opportunity. These can be very seductive, but you simply do not have the time or resources to follow every road.

The Idea in Action

Sandra Logan was the manager of training and development at a large corporation. Educated and experienced, she was well regarded by senior management and the people who attended her department's events. Her goals were to provide employees with the skills that would result in greater morale, productivity, and profits for the company. Research showed her methods worked, and the company stuck with them.

When the company hired a new director of human resources, to whom Sandra reported, one of his first moves was to rework the training curriculum. He waved Sandra off when she pointed out the proven success of her approach. She explained, also to no avail, that the staff was up on all the latest "fads" and routinely incorporated their best elements into existing programs. "People don't care about the content," he countered. "They want to work for a company with a progressive image. The seminars I want to add are popular nationwide." Sandra was overruled.

It wasn't long before negative feedback showed up in the "relevance" column of T & D's program evaluation forms. Employees joked openly about the new training. In one case, they didn't even have the hardware to run the software they were being trained to use. Morale took a dive. Some took the attitude that if the company wanted to waste money on useless training exercises, they were happy to "have the day off." Whole departments developed a collective paranoia that the changes in training meant job obsolescence. Many quit rather than be fired.

All in all, changing a system that was functioning well was a disaster. The new director moved on within a year, so the outcome had little impact on him. But for Sandra and the others in it for the long haul, it took years to reverse the damage, all because of the whimsy of one career transient.

For Reflection

How often do you vary from your original course when working on a project or task? How do you resist being tempted off course?

What has been your experience when you did decide to vary the course (other than when it was absolutely necessary)?

22
FINISH WHAT YOU START

If you don't finish what you start, you will be distracted by a mountain of unfinished business.

In More Depth

It is a sign of character and professionalism to live up to your commitments. It has been said that the most valuable employees are the ones who consistently do what they say they will. The same can be said of managers. Closing business gives people confidence in their leaders. It also inspires (and subtly demands) that they do the same.

Another angle on this is your own example of productivity and efficiency. The more "loose ends" you have in your work style, the greater the likelihood of mistakes or poor work. A pile of unfinished work creates a situation in which you lack focus and drain your mental energy.

The Idea In Action

Gary was a busy entrepreneur/manager and sometimes a writer. He was full of great ideas, and he had the ability to get people excited about his ideas, be they customers, investors, publishers, whoever. Gary was a person people envied. Everyone felt he was really going somewhere.

Over the years, however, Gary fell into a pattern of taking on too many projects and not finishing what he started. He would promise to read employees' reports and respond to their issues, typically saying,

"I've started on that. I'll finish it over the weekend and get back with you." He rarely did. Similarly, he would promise investors that he would meet project deadlines and objectives, but he rarely did this either. He would promise editors to finish an article they had commissioned, but failed to deliver on this too. His desk was buried in unfinished business and his list of phone calls to be returned reflected concerns left dangling.

Gary became so bogged down, he started getting confused about what he needed to be doing. He was losing the respect of his employees and customers. His avocation of writing was suffering as well. Worst of all, from his perspective, he was losing enthusiasm for his work. He loved to create and build, but found himself unable to do so because he seldom finished what he started.

One day, Gary "got the spirit" and decided that he just had to tie up some of the loose ends. He vowed not to initiate any new projects until the old ones were handled. This was tough, but he knew it was necessary to survive. He enlisted the help of several trusted employees and colleagues. "Be hard on me; keep me on track," he told them. The key was that he was now committed to completing things. That dedication and setting up a support team to help him saved the day.

He still struggles with the temptation to jump into new things before finishing old business, but Gary has matured and disciplined himself...and his friends still help keep him on track.

For Reflection

What projects on your desk are unfinished?
What one thing should you finish today?
How much mental energy would you gain if your desk were cleared?

23

ADOPT A CODE OF CONDUCT

Establish and communicate a code of conduct for your organization. Be clear about expected professional and work standards.

In More Depth

People want to know what is expected of them. Tell them. Have a code of conduct which explains what the company (and you) expect of people.

You develop a code of conduct to generate unity, not to create clones. When people know what the organization believes is professional behavior, it becomes their choice to go along or not. If they do, they become united in effort. If not, then action needs to be taken.

The code is to be work-focused and is not meant to interfere with an employee's personal life. It is okay, however, to address outside activities that can impinge on work performance, such as drug use or political activity. For example, "XYZ, Inc. does not profess or endorse any political viewpoint. Employees should not use the company name in connection with political activities." Be specific about everyday kinds of issues, too. If playing music on the job is a problem, say so. If keeping lunch to an hour is important, include it. If keeping a neat work environment is a priority, write it down. Be thorough.

Finally, stay flexible. Include language that allows input from others, for example,"We agree to abide by all established policies and procedures. Any disagreements will be brought to the attention of someone with the authority to review the policy and make a decision. Once a policy is reviewed, we agree to abide by the outcome of the review."

The Idea in Action

Jack was transferred from the accounting department in Houston, to another division in Chicago. In seven years at Houston, he had turned the operation from mediocrity to one of the country's best.

In Chicago, he learned he was following a laissez-faire manager, who let people do what they wanted. There was little teamwork. Employees felt they knew what was needed, and some were casting the department in a very poor light. Jack met with staff and learned that they were frustrated with the situation, too. There was a general sense that things were more difficult than necessary.

With the input of his staff, Jack put together a code of conduct, which he had printed and displayed in the accounting area. The objective was to provide a stable, structured environment for employees.

Some people loved it. Others hated it. Jack entertained all feedback, but he held to the code. A few people couldn't adjust and left. In one case Jack had to remove a person who refused either to cooperate or to leave. Overall, however, professionalism, cooperation, and productivity improved dramatically. Whenever anyone "broke the code," someone else would usually speak up. Rather than spend so much effort managing, Jack let the code manage whenever possible.

For Reflection

Does your team know what conduct is expected?
Do you make it clear what the code of conduct is for your team?
Is your code fair and productive? (Is it due for a review?)

24

KNOW HOW YOUR EMPLOYEES THINK

Find out your employees' thought processes. The method by which a person arrives at his or her conclusions is the basis for support or retraining. Don't assume you know those methods.

In More Depth

It is a mistake to assume employees will arrive at the same conclusions that seem obvious to you as manager.

We all have our own thought processes. Even if we reach the same conclusion, it is very likely that we reached it differently. You can easily see how this aspect of human nature can cause problems. In one instance, our thought processes can lead us to the same conclusion. At other times, we may end up miles apart. Consequently, people get upset.

If you ask about and understand employees' thought processes, you can correct errors or coach them more effectively. You also gain insight into their working styles and discover ways to make them more productive in the future.

The Idea in Action

Vaughn E. was a very busy manager. When a new salesman came aboard, she explained the company's products to him (a line of calculators), some of their key features, and how they differed from some competitive calculators. "Now go sell!" she said.

After several weeks, she noticed he wasn't selling many calculators. When she asked him about it, he indicated that they only seemed to appeal to young people like himself. Other sales reps were having success selling to people of all ages.

That night, Vaughn was struck by something she had heard at a management seminar on employee motivation. She remembered someone teaching, "If you have an employee who is not performing, explore whether the employee suffers from lack of ability, lack of will, or lack of training." Clearly, her salesman had the will and the ability, so the only option left was that he needed training. She didn't like that option because the responsibility fell back on her, but she was honest enough to accept it and do something about it.

She asked him to explain what went through his head when he was in a selling situation. His answers made her realize she had taught him the technical features of the product, and even about sales strategy, without addressing the product's benefits to an array of users. She also realized his thought process limited him to thinking in terms of how the product would help him, and therefore how to sell to people like himself. Seeing these understandable, unavoidable limitations in his thinking allowed her to develop him into one of her top sales people.

For Reflection

How does your "best" employee think?

How does your "worst" employee think?

When developing people, how do you guide them, by their thought processes or only by the outcome of their thoughts?

The Big Picture

25

KEEP THE BIG PICTURE IN MIND

Look beyond what it takes to get your job done. Try to understand how the entire organization works.

In More Depth

To be most effective as a manager, try organizing your knowledge into three timeframes: past, present, and future. To use a building metaphor, the past is the foundation you're building upon; the future is the blueprint for development; and the present is the actual work.

You must know the past to comprehend the foundation you are building upon. You wouldn't believe how many managers just start trying to build without first checking the larger context for their actions.

You must also be aware of what is going on now. How are your systems working? Who are your customers? How is morale? How is quality? What's the competition doing? How's the economy affecting you?

As for the future, you need to have an awareness of where you and your organization want to go. What are your goals? What is your vision? This is your blueprint. You have to see the structure of the future in order to guide the workers in the present.

The Idea in Action

Norman S. was hired as the new manager of a community convention center in a large southwestern city. He was young and confident, perhaps a little too confident. He didn't have much time between ending his old job and beginning the new one, but he reasoned that when he arrived he could motivate his staff by walking in the first day and presenting his grand plan for revitalizing the convention center and expanding the scope of operations—a sole focus on the future.

Norm was disappointed that his plans weren't met with rousing enthusiasm, but only polite acquiescence. Yet he was determined and bulled his way forward. He met little resistance from the staff, but he did sense a sort of begrudging hesitancy, which he shrugged off.

He ran into obstacles with local officials, members of the chamber of commerce, and a few of the major conventions. His sense that something was wrong grew stronger. Not one for self-pity, he seldom let a staff member see him in a down mood. One day, however, he got caught by his tough-as-nails, streetwise secretary.

She sat him down and gave him a tough-love, motorcycle-riding granny talk, as follows: "Norm, you didn't give a damn how we do things around here—the problems and the opportunities—so you stepped into the problems. You didn't care what we thought or how things worked in this city, and now you're paying the price. Sure, you should have ideas and be a leader, but you should have done some homework about us, how we've operated, our vision. You're a good person who can correct those mistakes. So get your butt out there and do it."

She had him. There wasn't a lot he could say.

For Reflection

What are the five most important parts of your organization's history?

How would you describe the situation today with regard to competition, morale, product quality, technology, and impact of economy ?

In under 100 words, describe your blueprint for your organization's future.

26
FEW DECISIONS ARE FOREVER

Events, people, values, and environments change. Each decision lasts only until the next one is made.

In More Depth

Make decisions, but be willing to change direction when the situation warrants. Since decisions, policies, and procedures are usually based on the information available at a given moment in time, it is appropriate to reexamine them when you have additional data.

The questions to ask yourself are: (1) Does my decision move us toward our goals? (2) Would altering the decision significantly improve a previous decision (not a minor or incremental one)? (3) Would altering the decision cause problems for anyone or for any process? (4) What are the consequences or problems if I do not change?

The Idea in Action

Raphael H. was the sales manager for a branch of a cellular phone company. He had been in the position for two years and was reasonably successful. There was little reason for him to change how he operated except that he decided he wanted to be more than "reasonably" successful. He decided to explore ways to improve on his success.

First, he listed his major decisions, written and unwritten, such as: I expect each salesperson to call on six people per day. Everyone is expected to have her or his paperwork done at the end of each day. The northwest side of town is the best market for us to pursue. I'll hire only young, attractive sales associates. Since Raphael was very rigorous with himself, the list was quite lengthy. For good measure, he added all the procedures he had initiated.

He then asked himself and some of his staff if these decisions were still valid. To his surprise, he found that about one in five was questionable. In other words, changing these decisions could lead to substantial improvement.

Raphael was wise enough to know that people sometimes resist change and that changing 20 percent of how his group did business all at once would cause chaos. So he prioritized his list and began systematically addressing the most critical issues and also concentrating on those decisions which would yield the most in terms of productivity.

Having done this, Raphael decided to review all his decisions on a regular basis, in addition to being willing to examine them as needed.

For Reflection

What three decisions need to be reviewed this week?

What are some of your unwritten decisions (the ones you carry around in your head)?

When was the last time you rigorously examined your policies and procedures?

27

EXAMINE YOUR PERCEPTIONS

Change is a constant. Adjust with it. If you don't change, the organization won't move forward, or it may move forward without you.

In More Depth

We all see things in our own way. That's natural. The problem comes when our perceptions do not reflect reality.

Let's take an example. You hired a young salesperson right out of college. You gave her the first job she ever had. She was inexperienced but tried hard. Since you don't get involved with sales (your district manager handles that), you still perceive her as a young greenhorn, even though it has been three years since you hired her. A sales manager position opens up. Her name is presented. You pass on her because of your perception, only to learn a month later that the competition has hired her because she was one of your top salespeople.

Examine your perceptions rigorously. Even if you were right on target when you first made the decision about something, things change. You cannot afford to operate with outdated or unsupported ways of seeing things.

Here's a list of categories in which managers tend to get stuck: seeing people for who they once were, not who they are today; seeing the market as it used to be, not how it is; seeing the competition as static; and seeing yourself and your company as you were, as opposed to how you are now or should be.

The Idea in Action

Sam Naylor founded his dry cleaning business as a young man in 1956. He opened in the corner of a small shopping center, the only one in a small city of 31,000. He worked hard and was somewhat of an autocrat with employees. There were two other cleaners in the city.

The Naylor shop earned a good reputation and experienced success enough to open a second location in the early 1960s and a third in the 1970s. The city grew to approximately 90,000 by 1990.

Mr. Naylor wanted to retire and turn the business over to his son, but had some serious disagreements with him. Junior thought the business needed to change in order to be viable. He had research data showing Naylor's had lost market share. Dad didn't want to change. "If it ain't broke, don't fix it!" was his motto. He pointed out that he was still making good money.

Junior pointed out that the competition had modernized; that good employees were being lured away because they were treated as "hired help" at Naylor's; and there were new services the public wanted which Naylor's did not provide.

Although Sam was stubborn, he couldn't dispute these things. He capitulated in the realization that the greater importance lay in a smooth succession and letting the next generation start making strategic decisions.

For Reflection

When was the last time you rigorously examined your perceptions about your organization?

How have your perceptions changed with changing situations?

In one sentence each, how do you view your competition, your customers, and your employees? Does this reflect the reality of today?

28

YOU WON'T ALWAYS WIN

There will be times when you do everything right and still don't get the desired results.

In More Depth

It's frustrating, but things don't always turn out the way you want them to, even when you do everything right. Life is uncertain, and management often is more an art than a science. Don't let it get you down, and certainly don't let it keep you from trying.

Often you'll look at a situation and ask yourself, "What should I do?" You'll bring into play all your education, training, and experience, not to mention your intuition. Based on all known factors, you'll make what is obviously the best judgment. You're confident you are doing what is right to get you to your desired goal. Given the same circumstances, nine out of ten managers would make the same call. You'll act on your decision, and for whatever reason, it won't work out.

Does that mean you made a mistake in your judgment? No. Does it mean you were only dreaming, that your goal wasn't realistic? No. Sometimes it just means that we live in a random universe in which things don't always work out. It hurts to lose. And we can certainly work to avoid future mistakes. The lesson remains: You won't always win.

Here's hoping you win more than you lose. That's the real definition of a winner. Be skeptical of people who say they have always won at everything they tried. Either they're lying or they haven't tried to do much.

And look at the flip side. Sometimes even when you mess up, things still turn out. You learn something unexpected that becomes a breakthrough opportunity.

The Idea in Action

Dr. Utiger wanted to open a second clinic on the other side of town to serve patients in their own neighborhood and expand his medical practice. He knew he was a good doctor, but he was aware there were limitations in his business understanding, even though his practice in his first location was successful. Some would say it was very successful.

He was wise enough to recognize that despite his success, he needed to learn more about business and about expanding existing businesses. He read books on starting, owning, and operating small businesses. He took a class in entrepreneurship at the local college. He even went so far as to hire an expert in setting up medical practices to consult with him.

He did everything right: read books, followed his consultant's advice, worked with bankers and marketing agents, did his research, and executed the plan to perfection. A year later, he had to close his second location because it was losing money and draining his time.

What did he do wrong? Nothing. It just didn't work. Armchair critics can speculate all they like. That's irrelevant. It simply didn't work.

For Reflection

Are you able to accept a defeat as a normal part of work and life?

Are you blaming yourself for a failure? Can you let go of that feeling and move on without it negatively affecting you?

Think back to a previous loss or failure. How did you overcome it? What did you learn from it?

29

KNOW WHY YOUR ORGANIZATION EXISTS

Be specific about your purpose. Hold rigorously to that course. Avoid trying to be everything to everybody.

In More Depth

You need to know what you are trying to do. Then you need to communicate it. If your purpose (mission, vision, whatever the current buzzword) is too vague, people will assume you aren't sure what it is, that it isn't important, or that *they* are supposed to decide what it is.

Let's say your mission is to get from Los Angeles to New York City. You could communicate that as, "We're going to New York." or you could say, "Eastward, ho!" Both are correct. Both get you going in the right direction. But only one gets you to the real destination. You can imagine how much more effective it is if everyone is focused on a specific destination and knows what it means to arrive.

Once you have embarked upon a mission, resolve to hold that course and weather all storms. To use a sailing metaphor, you have to adjust to the winds and the waves, but to reach your destination, you pick a fixed point in the distance and don't take your eyes off it. This doesn't mean never changing your plans. It does mean not changing without a powerful reason.

Finally, once you set sail, don't get sidetracked by unscheduled "ports of call." Certainly there will be some intriguing distractions along the way. Keep your purpose in focus. You have limited resources (money, time, people). You simply must decide where best to deploy them.

The Idea in Action

Lonestar Duds had a corporate mission: to provide the best men's clothes possible in a moderate price range to the Texas population via company stores in mall locations. Then the company president, Lynn Z. decided to rewrite it.

He decided the company needed to expand its horizons, often a good idea for business. He wanted the new statement to be simple and profound. It read: To provide apparel to the largest possible population at a profit.

Lynn thought this would offer more opportunities: a variety of clothing, not just men's; expansion outside of Texas; both high- and low-priced merchandise; and the possibility of free-standing stores and licensing agreements.

His buyers took it as carte blanche to buy anything they thought might sell at a profit. Although they had not saturated Texas, the development people started exploring sites in Louisiana, Oklahoma, and New Mexico. His real estate people immediately began developing a prototype for a free-standing store.

Any one of these ideas might have been okay, and, technically speaking, they did fulfill the new corporate mission. But together, all set free to find their own direction, they spelled chaos.

For Reflection

Do all your employees know your organization's mission?

Are you absolutely clear about the mission? Are you "holding the course"?

How is your corporate mission communicated in your daily management activity?

30

THERE ARE FEW "RIGHT" ANSWERS

Develop a tolerance for ambiguity. The world is not black and white. Management is as much an art as a science.

In More Depth

Perhaps in mathematics or in physics there are "right" answers. However, that luxury doesn't exist in the world of management—that is, interactions involving people.

If you view a management decision through a mathematical model, you see that the outcome is dependent upon the variables in the equation: People change, competition changes, products change, the environment changes, financial conditions change, and so forth. Thus the outcomes are not certain.

As a manager you must learn to be comfortable with that ambiguity. You should investigate and study to take as much uncertainty out of the equation as possible, but you cannot eliminate all uncertainty or risk. You will be forced to make many subjective decisions.

At some point, make your best decision. See how it plays. If it's right, enjoy it, but don't be seduced by its success. Other decisions may not play out as well. That's life in management.

The Idea in Action

Brigitte was a stickler for details, demanding that people do things "right." Working in a technical field (accounting), she became comfortable with the illusion that there were always right answers.

Getting promoted into management, therefore, caused her greater than usual anxiety. Now, she had to manage people, make projections on qualitative as well as quantitative data, and deal with corporate politics.

When budgeting, for example, it was easy to come up with a figure that represented what her people could reasonably accomplish, but getting to that figure was a different proposition. At first, Brigitte threatened firings all around if they fell short. There was a flurry of activity by everyone, but when the smoke cleared, productivity had actually declined, and it was impossible to tell who was at fault.

Fortunately for Brigitte, she had a sympathetic boss who understood the human element in business and suggested that less threatening tactics might yield better results. Thankful for the humane treatment, Brigitte passed it on, and the next year's results looked much better. She was learning the difference between "best" and "right."

For Reflection

Are you willing to live with the ambiguity in management decisions?
At what point do you accept a "best" decision versus a "right" decision?
How do you deal with the gray area in decision making?

31

EMBRACE QUALITY

Concentrate on and produce quality in everything. The memory of quality brings people and money back.

In More Depth

You can always find a way to do something cheaper and easier. This often makes good business sense…unless it compromises quality. There was a time when we in America embraced a "disposable" mentality with regard to our products and services. That is no longer viable. Nowadays, quality is vital. It's the price of admission into business, and you must focus on it in every aspect of your organization: product, service, management, human resources, all of it. The payoff may not be immediately apparent, but it will be much more sustained.

It is not enough to look at the competition and match its quality standards. To develop a commitment to quality, you must look beyond a current standard and focus instead on a constant process of rigorous examination and improvement. The most successful companies—and this includes nonprofits—will focus on hiring the best people and providing the best development opportunities for employees and management, so that they can provide the very best products and services.

The Idea in Action

Allen was hired as COO for a regional chain of quick-print shops. He had a reputation for being tough, but fair, and totally obsessed with quality.

The company was an early entrant in the "quick print" market and had established a good position. Allen was hired because the company was now losing market share and had lost its number one ranking.

As with any lucrative market, competition had followed, so some loss in the leader's market share was predictable. There was more to it, though. The company had become complacent with its service. It was considered no big deal to miss an occasional deadline.

It lagged in buying the latest technology, which its competitors now employed. It also failed to upgrade its shops to reflect a professional environment. And, it had done little employee and management development. Many employees were still working with skills used ten years ago, and management acted as though the company was still the undisputed industry leader and could manage the same way as before.

Allen quickly saw the problems. He investigated the competition to see what the market had accepted. He didn't stop there. He led the way throughout the organization with a commitment to quality in everything it did: product, service, and methods of delivery. He began a program to reevaluate everything the company did by applying the question: Is it possible to make this better?

He met resistance from some employees, but he persevered, and within two years the company had regained nearly a third of the market share it had lost. Its reputation improved significantly, all of which resulted in an increase 43 percent profits.

For Reflection

How would your describe your organization's commitment to quality?
What three aspects of your operation need quality improvement the most?
What are you willing to do to improve quality in your organization?

32

ONE BATTLE DOES NOT MAKE A WAR

Don't be afraid to lose a battle to win a war. Keep focused on your goal. Rarely is one event the end of the process.

In More Depth

Choose carefully which battles deserve your attention and resources. Then you can focus your efforts more effectively. Even when you are optimally focused, you may sometimes lose.

Sometimes it's best to retreat in order to win over the long term. A good general is one who knows when to pull back and plan to attack on another day. It would be foolish to sacrifice your resources when you see you're in a losing position. No long-range strategy rests on a single component of an action plan. If it does, the problem is in the plan.

Trying to win at everything every time is a mark of someone with an ego problem. While failure is not something anyone relishes, people who can't deal with temporary setbacks may be setting themselves up for an even bigger fall. You'll have failures. The real winners are the ones who learn from mistakes and move on.

The Idea in Action

Miranda A. recently became a junior staff lawyer for a large corporation. She had been drilled by her father on how tough life was. "It's a cold world. Only the fittest survive. Never back down or show weakness!" Those words echoed in her mind.

Of course, she felt a strong need to prove herself, and pretty soon had made a reputation as a "pit bull" attorney. She would respond aggressively to any person or situation that didn't go her way. Every issue received equal passion. Victory was everything.

Kay Elgin, corporate attorney, thought Miranda had promise, but was concerned about her ability to set priorities, allocate resources, and compromise if the situation called for it. Kay devised a scheme for trying to get the point across to Miranda.

One day in the cafeteria, Kay remarked, "I need someone for the Spurry deal. Who should I choose?" "I'll do it." Miranda answered. "Have you had any setbacks lately?" Kay asked. "None," came the proud reply. "Too bad," Kay retorted. "We mayhave to give away some points to get this contract." Miranda was perplexed.

Soon thereafter, Kay tried again. "We're looking for someone who can win the Bjorn case," she said. Miranda jumped up. "I'll have them begging to be let off," she boasted. "Well, I was thinking of working with them on a joint deal next year, and I don't want to alienate them," Kay said. "Maybe Lyle's a better bet for this one." Miranda was crestfallen.

Not long after, Kay met Miranda in the hallway. She asked her if she thought she had what it took to get a good settlement in the HiLee suit. Miranda fell silent (a good sign). After a bit, she said the words Kay had been waiting for: "What are our long-term goals for this one?" "Come into my office," Kay replied. "I'll fill you in."

For Reflection

How do you react to minor setbacks?

How do you determine which priorities deserve your attention and resources?

How would you convey the message of this rule to someone new to your team?

33

DON'T ALWAYS EXPECT A HAPPY ENDING

Discomfort can be both productive and a powerful incentive to change. There will be times when you will have to allow or create discomfort to achieve a happy ending.

In More Depth

We all like happy endings. We like it when movie characters fall in love and live happily ever after. Generally, in life, things do work out okay, but not always.

You must remember that you work with people, who are unpredictable and sometimes illogical. If we were machines, maybe things would work more predictably. Thankfully, we're not. We have the gift of life. Along with that gift, however, comes uncertainty.

People's feelings get hurt; people misinterpret things; people sometimes fail in good judgment; people are fallible. Sometimes people get sick and can't finish a job; sometimes they move to other parts of the country, leaving you stranded on a project; sometimes they don't agree and sabotage your plans.

You have to be willing to accept unhappiness or at least some unhappy interactions in order to improve the situation at work. People may need to "duke it out" to get clarity and truth into a situation. An idea may need to be tried, even if you suspect it will cause problems, if only to let a trainee learn what won't work. Accept that discomfort may be necessary to make things work in the long run.

The Idea in Action

Jasmine was hired to manage the billing office of a temporary services agency. She supervised nine people and was told when hired that they didn't work well together. She wanted to be friendly to her staff and liked by them, so she went out of her way to be friendly, helpful, clear in her directions, and supportive of their efforts.

Despite that, she noticed that they fought, were often uncooperative, and certainly did not go out of their way to help each other when the workload was uneven. This frustrated her. She needed to get the work out, and she preferred having a pleasant work environment. To get the work done on time, she had to resort to authority to force cooperation and work output. She knew this couldn't last if she didn't also force the issue of a pleasant workplace.

Although she disliked confrontation, she insisted everyone sit down for a serious "heart-to-heart," putting their feelings on the table to get to the root of the conflict. Reluctantly at first, but then warming, people spoke out on what was bothering them. Some comments were painful to hear. Others were humorous once they had been acknowledged to the group.

The situation improved somewhat and people began to express their concerns more openly and sensitively to the others. It took about six months, but eventually they became more cooperative and productive.

For Reflection

What situation at work is causing you discomfort now?

Are you and the other people involved being honest with each other about your feelings?

What first step could you take that (while being uncomfortable) might start the process of making it better?

Team Building

34
KNOW YOUR WORKING STYLE

Be aware of when your style serves the organization and when it doesn't. When it is inappropriate, change or leave.

In More Depth

We all have a "work style." Hopefully, it's been refined into something professional and effective. If you don't know it, ask at least five people who will be honest with you to describe your style, along with its strengths and weaknesses. You may even want to use anonymous questionnaires.

There are times when you will need the flexibility to shift your style to fit the needs of the situation. For example, you may be a very focused, assertive, and direct person who sees efficiency and productivity as the most important aspects of managing an operation. There are times, even in the most efficient organizations, when a more sensitive approach is needed. Let's take a vivid example: A popular employee is killed in a car accident. Is this the best time to dwell on productivity goals? Or do allow time for grieving and healing?

On a more permanent basis, you will want to continuously develop your capacity to adapt your style to fit the changing economic, legal, and global climate. The autocratic style seen 20 years ago will not only create morale problems, but probably cost you legal fees to defend yourself. A "flower-power" style that lets employees do what they like and assumes all will work out can be equally devastating in today's competitive environment. As in nature, adapt or die.

The Idea in Action

Brad was a 12-year employee with an electronics firm. He was well liked as an employee, and then as a project leader. He always tried to do what management wanted, and he tried to please his colleagues as well.

When he was promoted to manager, he found that not only was he not enjoying his job, but people were not as friendly toward him. In addition, he felt great internal conflicts in trying to please all the different constituencies: boss, employees, other managers, customers, and so on.

An organizational consultant friend advised him that his style might not be what the organization needed right now. She suggested he ask seven people in the organization, whom he trusted, to give him honest feedback about his working style—what worked about it and what didn't.

Brad did this and was surprised to discover that his greatest strength as an employee was a weakness as a manager. His desire to accommodate and make everyone happy was very valuable as an employee, but as a manager, he needed to provide more direction and stand his ground more.

He adapted his style and was very successful. It wasn't easy at first, but it made him a better manager and helped the organization.

For Reflection

How would you describe your working style? How would others describe it?

What one aspect of your working style could be improved?

In what situations would adapting your style prove beneficial?

35

KNOW YOUR TEAM MEMBERS

Get to know the strengths and weaknesses of your people. Use this information to improve results.

In More Depth

We all have strengths and weaknesses. A good manager concentrates on bringing out each employee's best side and combining those strengths so they complement each other. Someone may have strong interpersonal skills, another may be very good analytically, and yet another may be good at seeing long-range possibilities.

Since no one person can have all the skills needed to successfully operate any organization, you need to mold your team in a way that makes use of these skills. Your real challenge as a manager is to find or create ways to blend these various strengths. That is no small matter.

You must begin by knowing your team members. When you know people, you learn what motivates them—and what demotivates them. You learn how they interact with certain people and under certain conditions. You pay attention to their working style, how they get things done. Only with this kind of information can you get the most out of all people, and merge their talents to get the most out of the team.

The Idea in Action

Sonia T. was hired as the executive director of a volunteer community service organization, primarily retirees. Managing a volunteer organization is tough in itself, but working with retirees, who were very independent-minded to say the least, was a monumental task. Sonia knew results depended on careful coordination of the strengths of her team members.

Since she had a large corps of volunteers, she concentrated first on the 8 project coordinators, who managed all the other volunteers.

In the first month she held two 30-minute talks with them individually. Thereafter, she held weekly meetings with the whole group. She recognized that this was not much time—six direct contacts each of them, plus any informal ones. But since the purpose was to get to know them, what motivated them, and how they interacted, this was sufficient time to get a very good feel for them.

She then proceeded to make assignments accordingly, matching people's skills to the demands of their projects. People who were good at schmoozing were assigned to fundraising, for example. People who did not work particularly well in groups were put in less interactive roles.

Taking their cue from Sonia, the coordinators got to know their volunteers too. Making use of people's best talents and accommodating their preferences whenever possible worked quite well. The organization thrived. Morale was higher, which led to greater productivity and greater service to the community. And the organization was able to get more mileage out of a limited budget.

For Reflection

What are the strengths and weaknesses of the people who report directly to you?

If you were playing a strategy game against shrewd and highly organized opponents, how would you organize your team differently than it is organized today?

Have you ever had a boss who really knew the employees and used that knowledge? Was it effective?

36

DEFINE ROLES CLEARLY

Different situations require different roles: decision maker, information giver, leader, follower, ambassador, team player, individualist. Define and communicate your role and the roles of your team members.

In More Depth

Sometimes you need to be a leader; other times demand that you be a follower. There are times when you need to be an outspoken firebrand, and others when you need to be the consummate diplomat. Different situations require different responses. The ability to be flexible and know what role to take in response to a specific situation will distinguish you from less-successful managers.

Learn which role is required for each situation. Then simply flex your style to meet the need. Managers who maintain one style for all interactions are limited in their options and, therefore, in their success. They may feel they are sacrificing something of themselves in order to change. In reality, you lose if you develop a reputation for being rigid and inflexible.

When working with employees, tell them what roles you expect them to play. If they are sitting in a planning meeting, let them know that they are there to provide information, not necessarily to make decisions. When you send them to meet others outside the organization, empower them to be ambassadors—or tough negotiators—as the case may require. Tell them what you expect, and you're much more likely to get what you want.

The Idea in Action

Bart L. was vice president of sales for a large financial services company. He could be a motivator with his managers and salespeople, or a tough "I'm in charge" type when discipline was called for. He was a team player with other senior managers, and a follower when he was with the president or the board. He was a diplomat with angry customers, but could dig in when negotiating a contract.

Bart had a problem with one of his new managers. Roy had been a successful salesman. His personal style was outgoing and dominant. In management meetings, he tried to out talk the others. He did the same thing with irate customers. He just couldn't stand losing. His staff meetings usually ended with people agreeing with him just to get out of the room. The final straw came at a companywide meeting to solicit ideas for new products. The guy was so overbearing that the president told Bart something needed to be done about this fellow.

Recalling a time when he was less experienced, Bart decided to give Roy the benefit of the doubt. He called Roy in to explain the problem and the need to play a variety of roles. Otherwise, his effectiveness would suffer. Bart knew he had a problem when Roy resisted changing what "came natural to him." Although Bart gave him a few more chances, he ultimately had to discharge Roy because he was damaging the company.

For Reflection

Are you able to flex your style to fit different situations?
Do you tell team members what their roles are in various situations?
How do you coach someone to change his or her style to fit the situation?

37

MAKE REQUESTS INSTEAD OF ISSUING ORDERS

Unless you are in the military, orders are usually not received well. People want to be asked. A request invites participation and cooperation.

In More Depth

Would you rather be asked or told to do something? The answer is obvious. Ordering people around creates a "me boss, you slave" sort of feeling. Psychologically, it revives memories of having to do what your parents said. It makes you feel childish.

When you ask someone to do something, it enables that person to feel like a participant in making the organization work. People who feel valued are more productive and cooperative. Don't be afraid they'll think you're weak. They know you have formal authority and can use it at will. They will respect you more if you use it sparingly.

In today's world, good workers are quite mobile. If future predictions of a shortage of quality workers come true, it will become even more important to make employees feel part of the team. Asking rather than telling is one way to do that.

The Idea in Action

As a successful sales manager for a bedding company, David D. was adept at using his sales skills to make his reps feel important. They respected him in turn and followed his direction, not because he demanded it but because they wanted to.

Dave was told he would be promoted to marketing director in six months. His assignment in the interim was to choose and develop his own replacement. He chose Larry, who had an excellent record in sales and had held a management position prior to joining the company.

Over the next two months, David watched in disbelief as quiet, efficient Larry turned into a total jerk. He delighted in giving orders, "busting people's chops," and reminding everyone he was boss. Needless to say, the salespeople were less than excited about this behavior.

David felt responsible. He had to groom a replacement, and he knew Larry was capable if he could be convinced of how self-destructive his behavior had become. Then a light went on, and David decided to take a chance. He was still Larry's boss, and still had time to turn things around. For the next three weeks, he made Larry's life hell, issuing orders, making last-minute demands, arbitrarily making him do things over.

At first, Larry thought it was a joke, but as life grew more miserable, he was appalled at how good old Dave could let power go to his head. Finally, he couldn't stand it anymore, and he protested Dave's treatment of him. It was the opening David had been seeking. "How's it different from your treatment of your people?" he shot back. And that one line was all it took. Larry knew instantly he had been set up, and he was simultaneously ashamed and relieved. He had noticed the mounting insubordination, and he realized with embarrassment that he was the cause of what could have become his own downfall.

For Reflection

What percent of the time do you demand? What percent do you ask?
How do you resist the temptation to "issue orders"?
Can you invite participation and cooperation without issuing orders?

38

PROVIDE FEEDBACK, BOTH FORMALLY AND INFORMALLY

People need to know what's expected and how they will be evaluated. Feedback should be timely, regular, constructive, and honest.

In More Depth

Not only do people *need* to know, they *want* to know what to do and how well they're doing it. Positive feedback makes us want to repeat a behavior. Negative feedback makes us want to eliminate the behavior. How simple. Yet few managers use these powerful tools.

Feedback must be given so that people feel you're on their side. The key is in your intent. With positive feedback, the idea is to help through reward and praise, not to manipulate. It's not a trick to gain greater output. Negative feedback is telling people what they're doing wrong and showing them a better way. Again, do it to help, not with the attitude that they are bad or that you "caught them." Reinforcement of any kind is more meaningful and valuable when done soon after the behavior occurs.

Feedback should be given both formally and informally. You'll get far more chances to do it informally. When someone is doing something well, tell them them! If they're doing something that needs correcting, speak up immediately! Formal evaluations, by contrast, require that people know what's expected of them. It's unfair to evaluate employees when they don't know the criteria for measurement. It's your job to let them know.

The Idea in Action

Jackie W. is the operations manager in a discount department store. She is very successful and is held in high regard by the employees and senior management. That wasn't always the case.

When Jackie was first promoted to manager, she felt the way to make her mark was to find all the flaws in the systems and people. She would keep notes and tell people what they were doing wrong in their yearly evaluations. Because they hadn't been told exactly what was expected, they felt spied upon.

Jackie was hurt when she noticed people seemed to hide from her. She was even more upset disturbed when she heard someone say how much he disliked her. She liked people and was just trying to do her job.

The district manager, a good coach/counselor, noticed Jackie's problem and invited her to talk about it. Relating some of her own successes and problems, she gave Jackie this advice: "Tell your people what's expected. Give lots of feedback. Praise them when you see them doing something well. Help them by letting them know what they can do to improve. Give them a regular forum to give and get feedback. Do this honestly and in a way that convinces them you truly want to help, and you will have a long, rewarding career.

Jackie tried it. She had to earn back their lost trust, but once this was done, she was amazed at the respect and friendliness she received.

For Reflection

How do you provide your staff with informal feedback?

Does you staff know the criteria by which they're being evaluated?

How do you search for the good things your people do, and how do you provide feedback for these good actions?

39

REWARD GOOD PEOPLE AND GOOD PERFORMANCE

Spend your time, money, and attention on your good people. Don't inadvertently reward poor performance.

In More Depth

Remember the old 80-20 rule? Eighty percent of your results come from 20 percent of your people. Any successful organization relies on this top 20 percent. You should know who yours are. If you don't, find out. Then find ways to let them know they're valued.

Even when you know who they are and how important they are, it's tempting to take your stars for granted. Sometimes you just get swamped dealing with the other 80 percent—usually handling problems. Sometimes managers feel these workhorses don't want any feedback. In reality, they don't mind help; it's just that they've been burned so often by poor management input, they've ceased expecting anything worthwhile. Another common mistake managers make is to assume that piling on more work is a way of saying you're valued.

Put yourself in their shoes. When someone takes you for granted, what do you do? If you're like most people, you seek a situation in which you'll get the appreciation you think you deserve. When your stars leave for more money, recognition, or a better working environment, you lose. Recruiting is expensive, and the odds are 4 to 1 that you will not get another top producer. Not good.

The Idea in Action

Diane managed a cafe-bakery-catering company. The company made great food, was well known for its service, and was profitable. The catering brought in lots of money and was a good marketing promotion. It succeeded primarily because Diane always put one of her best people on each team. These team leaders loved what they were doing and went out of their way to make things work for the customers.

As business grew, Diane found herself dealing more and more with paperwork, handling employee problems, and scheduling. She began to neglect her team leaders, figuring that since they always did things so well, it freed her for more pressing matters. Besides, she thought, they're mature adults, they can fend for themselves.

Things began to decline; nothing alarming, but Diane could tell the company was losing ground. In the past six months, two top people had left to form their own catering business. Another went to work for a competitor.

Routine turnover, she thought, but by year's end, things had again become worse. She had lost two more good people…to other competitors this time. Interviewing replacements was cutting deeper into time spent with her best performers. Managing was getting ever more difficult.

Unfortunately, in this case, there is no happy ending. The vicious cycle continued until they closed the catering portion of the business. All those good people had taken other jobs or started their own catering businesses.

For Reflection

Who are the top five people (who really produce results) in your organization? How have you demonstrated your appreciation for them in the last month?

What percentage of your time is devoted to the top 20 percent of your employees, and what percentage to the bottom 80 percent?

40
CELEBRATE SUCCESS

People like to play and win. Celebrating successes, even small ones, reinforces winning behavior.

In More Depth

Some managers believe employees should be motivated by just doing their work and collecting their paycheck every two weeks. People will do that because they need the money to survive, but it does not produce motivated, productive people.

People like to win. They like to be on winning teams. Winners and winning teams celebrate. In the military they win medals and ribbons; in sports they win letters, trophies, and medals; in school they get gold stars and display their work on the wall.

Businesses and other organizations need to do this, too. Create a celebration whenever there is a significant success. It doesn't have to be elaborate or expensive: a short public success rally or posting a customer's thank-you letter on the employee bulletin board is a celebration.

For big successes, have a big celebration. Plan it into your budget. It is money well spent. Have award banquets, give out trophies, host group events, do anything that honors the person or the team responsible. Celebrations make work more fun and generate more winning events.

The Idea in Action

Lenny manages the community development department of a medium-sized city in the Midwest. He was chosen because the previous manager had retired and the city management believed Lenny would revitalize a department that had fallen into complacency.

One of the first things he did was to have a "celebration of the past." He told staff they would have Danish and coffee on Monday morning and spend a couple hours honoring past successes. The purpose was to bring closure, and he used the occasion to articulate new goals for the future.

Over the next six months he had to search pretty hard for successes that were leading to the new goals. New behaviors were slow in coming. If he noticed a worker who had done a nice report, or saw a letter from a citizen commending a staff person, he would highlight these successes in staff meetings and present small awards to these people.

The first time they exceeded their monthly goal of approvals on building developments, Lenny held a staff picnic. The staff played together, celebrating their success. When the group met its quarterly goals, Lenny wrote a letter of appreciation, which he framed, and put in the lobby with pictures of the staff who had participated. Suddenly that level of production became the standard. Celebrating created pride. And citizens who saw the awards assumed they were dealing with people who worked hard to help them.

Over the next year, as he monitored their progress, there were more celebrations. The cost was an insignificant part of his total budget, and productivity skyrocketed.

For Reflection

When was your last celebration?
What can you celebrate this month?
What kind of celebration would get your staff's attention?

The Day to Day

41

LEAVE THE OLD JOB BEHIND

Don't hang on to the old job when you are promoted. Make a clean break. Put it in the past.

In More Depth

Too often, when people are promoted, they try to do their old job from the manager's position. They may feel intimidated by the scope of the management position, so they regain some sense of competency by hanging on to all or part of their old job. After all, they probably got promoted because they were good at it, and everyone likes to feel they are really good at something.

They may also have really liked part of their old job, and hate to give up something they like. Every job has its good and bad points, its fun parts and its drudgery parts. Don't hang on because you like part of the old job. It's not fair to the new employee who took your place. Plus, you're taking away time that should be devoted to your new managerial duties. If you don't let go, you'll do half a good job of your old position and maybe half a good job of your new position—that's not a good bargain.

If you're hanging on to the old job because that's where you got your strokes for being very good, give it up. Admit your humanity, that it will take some time to become good at being a manager. Only then can you become a good manager.

The Idea in Action

Linda S. was promoted to manage the budget department at a nationally known charity. She had begun her career as a bookkeeper, worked her way up to accountant, and now was budget director. She was promoted in part because she was very knowledgeable about nonprofit accounting, was exacting in her work, and was always ahead of schedule. She took great pride in her work and was often heralded as an example of a great employee.

After the promotion, Linda seemed to pay a lot of attention to the work done by her replacement. Frequently she was quite critical when there was an error or if it took longer than she thought it should. Nor did she seem to pay as much attention to other people's work.

When the new person complained to her, Linda answered that she could fix it faster than explain it. "But how can I learn," the employee asked. "Maybe the job just isn't right for you. It takes someone very sharp to handle that position."

Linda didn't see the light until that employee requested a transfer and left the department. Now she had to do the old job, or get it done, out of necessity, not choice. It taught her the true meaning of getting work done through others. She also learned the value of retention of an employee over training from scratch.

For Reflection

What parts of your old job are you still doing (directly or indirectly)?

How many people can you name who "held on" after being promoted?

What do you imagine it is like filling the position of someone who is still holding on?

42
KNOW THE REAL ORGANIZATIONAL CHART

There is a difference between real power and organizational chart power. Discover who really makes the decisions in your company.

In More Depth

Most everyone knows that companies have an informal power structure that differs from the organizational chart. You must learn who has the real power and in what situations. Also, you must know how formal power and informal power relate. The formal authority figures are human just like you. We are all influenced by other people.

Informal power is often disguised. Those who advise a formal authority figure have power—spouses, lovers, relatives, and friends included. A person who has access to the formal authority's time (and ear) has power. A person who has specific knowledge and expertise critical to the organization has power. A union leader has power, but is not on the chart.

This doesn't deny the authority represented by the organizational chart, but the chart is only a skeleton. The lifeblood of an organization exists in the tissue which holds the skeleton together.

Ask. Listen. Observe. You'll soon learn where the influence exists. Once you know, use it the way you would use your knowledge of the formal organizational structure.

The Idea in Action

Harriet was hired as a management trainee at a large department store.

She knew that in addition to learning merchandising, ordering, and inventory control, she would need to develop good working relationships with people who had influence in the organization. She obtained a copy of the organizational chart, studied it, and began using that knowledge.

After several months, she noticed that although she worked through the chain of command as outlined in the chart and was competent, another trainee was having greater success getting things accomplished.

When she pointed this out to a trainee with whom she had become friends, he filled her in on the informal power structure: "Mr. T., our general manager, went to college with Ethyl, the accounting supervisor. He trusts her implicitly. So if I'm proposing a plan that will impact finance, I ask Ethyl to review it and give me her recommendations. That way, when it gets to Mr. T., it's certain to be approved. And Tom, our merchandising manager used to be a stockboy at this very store. When the warehouse is giving me the runaround, I get him to pull some strings with Joe, the warehouse manager. That's a sample of how things work."

Harriet didn't like what she heard. After all, she thought, why can't it just be clearcut like the organizational chart says? However, she did recognize the importance of the informal power structure and began using her new insight. It seemed the only way.

For Reflection

Can you draw the informal organization structure beside the formal organizational chart of your company?

What five people in your organization have more influence than what shows on the organizational chart?

Assuming that you recognize the importance of knowing the informal organizational chart, how can you use this knowledge?

43

SET UP SYSTEMS

Lay out procedures to manage daily operations. Do not make decisions on these matters other than to change established policies or procedures.

In More Depth

Design systems so you don't constantly have to make the same decision. A system is any established set of procedures, policies, or guidelines directing an employee to the proper decision. While some issues cannot be put into a system, most can. If a question, problem, practice, or event occurs repetitively, design a system to handle it.

When you design your systems, they should include contingencies and general exceptions. Where appropriate, they should also allow employees latitude to adapt to situations that don't fit the norm.

Once a system is established, make sure people use it, and don't fall into the trap of changing it too often. You only change the system or make an individual decision when there is a compelling need, when the system has failed to work adequately, or when new or additional information requires change. People like stability and they deserve it. Knowing and using the system helps them know when they are performing well.

As a manager, you don't have time to consider every issue. Setting up systems frees you to focus on issues that do require individual attention.

The Idea in Action

As nurse manager at a major hospital, Janet G. found herself overwhelmed with issues that needed a decision. It reached the point that she simply could not handle them all. Knowing that their situations were similar, she got the name of the nurse manager at another hospital and called to ask how she handled the problem.

The other nurse gave her some great advice: "You have to set up systems which allow your staff to make decisions based on the system. Rather than using you as their resource for every decision, the system becomes the resource."

That sounded logical, so Janet went back to her hospital and set out to systematize her work. She soon realized she didn't know where to start. She called her new friend again, who laid it out:

"For the next week, list the types of issues and problems that come across your desk. At week's end, look for trends or themes. Start with those. Design a system to address those. Then draft a sample method. Test and revise that sample system over the next month until it handles the vast majority of problems and issues. Then implement it. The following week, make another list of new issues and problems that arise. Draft another system. Test and revise. Implement. Continue this cycle, and within six months, you should eliminate 75 percent of the issues coming across your desk."

When Janet did this, she found that it not only freed her time for more important matters but also reduced her stress level, which had been rising due to the frenetic pace she was forced to keep without her systems.

For Reflection

What are the types of issues that routinely come across your desk?
If you had a system to handle these issues, how much time would you save?
What stops you from establishing systems in your work?

44

FIND AND DEAL WITH THE REAL PROBLEM

Managers often mistake surface issues for the real problem. Look beyond symptoms to find the underlying causes.

In More Depth

Often surface issues mask the real problem. Take the time and have the resolve to solve underlying problems not just surface issues.

This can be difficult. Busy managers are accustomed to "putting out fires." Demands on your time can be overwhelming, and tempt you to handle the most pressing problem. Unfortunately, you will encounter the same problem over and over unless you get to the core issue.

It's like a doctor prescribing an ointment to make a rash go away without discovering whether the rash is an allergic reaction to some substance. The rash may go away with the ointment, but it will be back when the person comes into contact with the substance again. The prudent doctor would seek out the offending substance and advise the patient to avoid it. The prudent manager finds the real problem and shows the work unit how to avoid further dysfunctional behavior.

The Idea in Action

Teddy Lavin was vice president of a small direct-marketing company. He was in charge of daily operations, including personnel. Business was good and growing. The company had a fine reputation, but Teddy noticed that the design unit was experiencing greater than average turnover.

He had faced a different situation in that unit every other week for several months. At first, an employee complained about the noise level. Teddy called in the manager and they issued a policy prohibiting radios at everyone's desk. Then someone complained because he couldn't find documents he needed. That, too, was easily solved with a new directive to "keep the place clean and orderly."

Several weeks later, two employees got into a shouting match. Both demanded to see Mr. Lavin, who discovered they were angry about a project assignment. Though he smoothed things over and they went away happy, Teddy had a gut instinct something else was wrong. That's when he checked the turnover figures.

When another employee disagreed with a work assignment and asked for an administrative review of the procedure, Teddy deferred a decision until he could spend time in the unit, which he scheduled that very week.

He found that the head of the unit, once a fine manager, had developed a drinking problem that was affecting his performance. All those issues were merely symptoms of this much larger underlying problem.

Teddy sought help from the Employee Assistance Program and pitched in at the unit while the manager was recovering. After treatment, things returned to normal. By addressing the real problem, complaints virtually stopped and turnover slowed to earlier levels.

For Reflection

What problem have you recently solved that could have been a symptom rather than the real problem?

What procedure do you use to discover the real problems when you face a symptomatic problem?

What do you think keeps managers from dealing with core issues?

45

YOU HAVE CHOICES

Know your options; you always have more than one. If you don't like them, keep looking.

In More Depth

You will make your best decisions when you choose from options rather than feeling forced into a certain position. Even if the "forced choice" is a good one, there is natural resistance to feeling compelled to do anything, and it may not receive your full commitment.

You always have a choice, if it is nothing more than doing something or not doing it. If you find you are feeling forced into a decision, or have only the yes/no option, the more productive approach is to generate additional options.

This is where creativity comes in. There are a number of creativity-enhancing techniques available to aid decision making: Brainstorming, creative visualization, taking the opposite approach, looking for similarities in unrelated things, and letting your unconscious mind work on the problem overnight as you sleep are just a few. You'll be surprised at the new opportunities you'll discover this way.

The Idea in Action

Dr. Herzog is the medical director for a large life insurance company. He reviews all medical situations presented on life insurance applications, consults with the company on all medical issues, and acts as the executive adviser to the president and board of directors on medical issues relating to the profitable sale of life insurance.

The company had a fine reputation of being a good corporate and community citizen. When insurance companies were rated by the public, it consistently received outstanding ratings in the category of serving people.

Dr. Herzog was faced with a dilemma. The marketing department had created a new policy that it wanted to market to people over age 65 (a time when the death rate begins to accelerate statistically). They wanted to do the unthinkable, from an actuarial perspective, and offer the policy to anyone over 65 regardless of their health status.

Herzog's dilemma was that he wanted to support marketing. Their research indicated a huge potential for this product and it would serve a needy community. But it would attract people who were very likely to be ill or infirm and skew the statistical base from which premiums were calculated. He felt his only option was to say no.

He decided to hold off on his directive until he could come up with at least one other option. The group brainstormed a creative compromise. If holders could be excluded from making claims for the first two years the policy was in force, the plan could be made to work. The outcome was a tremendously popular product with considerable profit potential for the company, all owing to a willingness to look for the positive option rather than automatically saying no.

For Reflection

How many options do you like having before you choose?

What process do you use to find more options in a given situation?

How would you describe the feeling of being trapped with only one option?

46

CULTIVATE A PERSONAL SUPPORT SYSTEM

The higher you go, the lonelier its gets. You need a personal support system.
Enroll a group of people whom you trust and who understand management.
Share the ups and downs of the job that no one else would understand.

In More Depth

Don't burden your spouse or best friends with work issues. There are
others in your same situation who would be happy to listen and share
their experiences. Depending upon the competitive environment within
your organization, you may have to create this personal support system
outside your company.

Enroll a group of people in your inner circle whom you trust and
who understand management. Then share your thoughts and war stories with people who will understand.

It's lonely at the top, or even in the middle. Being a manager, you are
privileged with confidential and sensitive information. Sometimes you
have to make unpopular decisions which affect people's lives. You may
need to fire people, and you will nearly always have competing and
conflicting voices vying for your attention and influence.

No one wants or needs to face the pressure alone. For your physical
and mental health, not to mention your sense of well-being and professional development, it is important to find people with whom you can
speak freely and safely, especially if they have some understanding of
management and leadership.

The Idea in Action

Brown recently became division manager. He began in the company as a summer intern and worked his way up. He liked his friends from the ranks, but now he was their leader.

He found senior management, employees, and his family and community making increasing demands on him. He felt the pressure and found himself isolated, angry, and frustrated. He used to go have a beer with the guys after work to talk out his problems, now he knew that was inappropriate. He was not comfortable enough with his boss to talk openly with him, and his close family members had their own problems.

One day at a stockholders' meeting, Brown found himself pouring out his soul to another division manager. Surprisingly, the guy seemed to welcome it. They resolved to get together for breakfast every Friday to talk. Over time, they invited several other colleagues on the same level to join them. And it was not long before the feelings of isolation and anger vanished.

For Reflection

Which people do you count on as your support system?

Do you try to "go it alone" too much?

What do you need to do to create a personal support system?

47

DON'T BE AFRAID TO ASK FOR HELP

Asking for help is a sign of wisdom and strength. No one goes through life or work alone.

In More Depth

Some people find it difficult to ask for help because they are afraid people will say no. That's possible, but it's much more likely they'll say yes.

Would you help someone out who asked you sincerely and needed your help on a short-term basis? Probably. Isn't it likely you would actually enjoy it, and that it might create a better working and friendly relationship with that person? That's a nice payoff for both parties, a payoff lost by denying others that opportunity. Obviously, this doesn't mean running to someone for help on every detail, but there are times when getting others' thoughts or involvement makes good sense.

You can't do it all. Sometimes you just become overburdened and need help to work out from under all the "to do" lists. Tell people the situation. Ask for help. You'll be surprised. They'll often say yes.

It's just good sense to bounce ideas off someone else. Another person can stimulate the creativity in you. You'll see new and different perspectives on issues, and you'll make better decisions for having considered more than just your viewpoint.

The Idea in Action

Dr. Lavoie was principal of a training and development consulting firm. She and her firm were well known for their seminars on management and leadership. Dr. Lavoie was an independent and assertive person who operated without much input from partners and staff.

Business was good and they were signing more contracts than usual. Several large contracts were new and required that Dr. Lavoie personally conduct the first training sessions so they could get off to a good start. These were also complicated contracts that had to be customized for the specific organization. Since Dr. Lavoie had secured these contracts from her professional network, she felt personally responsible for the delivery of the terms of the agreement.

She soon found herself buried in work, her regular work plus these additional burdens. Moreover, she wondered when she would have time to think through all the aspects of two major new workshops.

She strongly avoided asking for favors. Fortunately, one of her trainers sensed this and made the perfect comment over coffee one morning. "Dr. Lavoie," she intoned, "I wonder if we are acting with integrity in teaching our clients about certain managerial behaviors." "What?" Dr. Lavoie asked incredulously. "Well, I mean we don't model what we tell them. We tell them to gather the best minds and talents available to do a job, and not try to be the Lone Ranger and do everything themselves."

Dr. Lavoie got the message. With a sheepish grin, she acknowledged her failing and took action then and there to hand off some of the burden.

For Reflection

Would you be willing to help people if they asked and sincerely needed it?
What would stop you from asking them for help if you sincerely needed it?
How might seeking help allow you to operate better?

48
JUST SAY NO

When too much is asked of you, decline or renegotiate. Reorder priorities or drop lower-level tasks. Don't set yourself up for failure by overextending.

In More Depth

If you're any good at what you do, you will be asked to do more of it. If you're good at doing more of it, you will be asked to do still more. At some point you have to realize that you can only do so much. The point is to do what you do well.

Every successful manager has periods when there is too much to do. That is usually handled by working a few extra nights or having someone help you out, either by delegation or by asking a colleague to share the load. The problem is when you become chronically overwhelmed. Remember your first-grade math: $1 + 1 = 2$. The equation today is not much more complicated: $1 + 1 + \ldots + 1 = 24$, the number of hours in a day. If you add 1 to this, you simply must take 1 away so the equation still equals 24.

You must then learn the magic word "no." Despite its simplicity, many managers find it almost impossible to say no when it comes to additional responsibilities or projects. So try this exercise: Say out loud, "No, I am going to take care of myself, my family, and my friends, and do what I do well, instead of taking on more and more."

The Idea in Action

Nancy was a sales manager for a local department store, a devoted mother and partner, and president of the PTA. She was good at her work. She cared about her employees and her company. She also cared about the members of her church, the neighbors, parents and teachers of the PTA, a homeless shelter where she volunteered once a month, and a lot more.

She was so good at work that her boss kept asking her to be in charge of special projects. She agreed. She was so good at heading the PTA that other organizations sought her involvement. She was asked to be on special committees at the school. She was so good at being a wife and mother that her family took her a bit for granted and would think nothing of asking a friend to join them for dinner without telling her.

Nancy felt she was being pulled from all directions. She realized she was not doing everything to the level of quality she demanded of herself. Most important, she was not having any fun anymore.

Determined to get the fun back, she taught herself to say no. Her family and friends were shocked at first, but they found other ways to manage (and other busy people who agreed to be involved because they hadn't yet found the secret word).

Nancy got back her vitality and passion for her work, family, and causes…and she started having fun again.

For Reflection

How do you handle it when people ask you to take on more than you are comfortable with doing?

What could you do that would improve the way you handle such requests?

Is there someone you care about whom you may be guilty of overloading, because he or she has a hard time setting limits?

Technique

49

KNOW THE HISTORY OF YOUR ORGANIZATION

Be guided by your company's past, but don't let it run the organization. If it's negative, plan to overcome it. If it's positive, leverage it into more success.

In More Depth

Was it Santayana who said, "Those who don't learn from history are doomed to repeat it"? What this means for business is that success depends on your ability to see what caused past failures—like poor quality or bad management—and successes—like loyal customers or creative employees—and act to repeat the successes and avoid the failures.

It's not a good idea to come into an organization as a manager without learning its relevant history. Without it, you run several risks. You may fall into political traps that could be avoided by knowing past associations. Or you may not be prepared when an old issue arises from an employee, supplier, or customer. With it, you may see opportunities that would otherwise take you significant time to discover.

You don't have to do everything in accordance with past practice. Just acknowledge it as you would your own life: "All my past experiences—positive and negative—make me what I am today." Then you decide how to let it influence the present.

The Idea in Action

Thomas H. was recruited for the position of general manager for a regional food brokerage company. When he arrived at the new company, he called all employees together and gave a rousing talk about how this company could become a giant like his previous employer.

When his supervisors and employees offered to brief him on some aspects of the company's past, he dismissed it as backward thinking, "I don't care about the past; let's focus on future successes." He was trying to be inspirational.

Everyone went along because he was the boss. Occasionally, they would try to speak up, but he always cut it off as negativism. He therefore missed some key aspects of the company's history: a reputation for extra service, which resulted in great customer loyalty; subtle promises management had made to employees about future financial rewards (while not in writing, every employee had developed certain expectations); the sense of family, because it originally was a family business.

Thomas was unquestionably talented and brought good ideas from his former company, but he ran into considerable resistance when he cut costs—and the extra service; he tried, in vain, to head off a union attempt, because he ignored the concern about financial rewards and ignored very strong personal relationships which were not obvious on the surface.

It took a desperation move to save his job. He agreed to listen to the employees. He had done severe damage, so they were reluctant at first. But by finally listening, thereby honoring past relationships, he bought enough time to right things. It took two years to repair the damage. It could have been avoided with two days of learning.

For Reflection

How much of your company's history do you know?
How do you honor your organization's history?
What can be done about an organization that lives in the past? Does yours?

50

VISION MUST BE SUPPORTED BY ACTION

Vision builds on a firm foundation. There is no short cut from today to tomorrow. Goals are arrived at through planning, preparation, and execution.

In More Depth

Creating a vision and setting goals are both important tasks of leaders. They crystallize thinking, align the viewpoints of your team, and give people direction. But that's just the beginning. It is also the leader's responsibility to make the vision come alive. You must plan not just what will happen but how to make it happen.

First, consider how the goals interrelate. Then take each goal and formulate a step-by-step process to make it happen. Establish milestones and ways of measuring progress. Next, gather your resources—financial, physical, and human. Prepare your financial plan. Secure all the necessary physical resources—buildings, machinery, equipment, furniture. Then assemble your team and train and motivate it to achieve the goal.

Finally, having done all this preparation, move through your master strategy. Keep the milestones in view and don't forget to chart progress. You must follow up. Moving forward does not mean just sitting around thinking and talking about the plan.

The Idea in Action

Mary was elected to the presidency of the local school board in a large metropolitan area. The board was very visible in the community but was seen as being only moderately effective.

Every year the board elected a new president. For as long as anyone could remember, they had a retreat each year to set a vision and goals for the school system. This part was usually a lot of fun. The board members got to know each other, and they came away from the retreat feeling inspired. They always reported to their constituents that they were reenergized and anxious to move forward. The problem was that they never seemed to get much beyond this point. The enthusiasm waned and the public saw little new action coming from the board.

Mary was determined to break this cycle. Instead of having the retreat (which lasted a full day) focus totally on vision and goal setting, she set the morning aside for this, and she devoted the afternoon to planning methods for achieving each goal which supported the vision.

They then agreed to meet for one hour each month to monitor each step of the action plan they had created. They were each assigned a particular task; they set deadlines; and they decided upon and procured the resources necessary to achieve each goal. Mary took on the task of holding people to their commitments about the plans and either helped, coached, or cajoled all the members individually as they worked on their specific projects.

Mary was reelected until she finally said she wouldn't do it anymore. When she stepped down, she was hailed as the most successful president the board had ever had.

For Reflection

Where do your plans stand now for this year's goals?
What method do you use to track your action plan?
How do you, as the leader, make sure the vision is achieved?

51

STAY IN TOUCH

Occasionally go into the trenches. Don't ever lose your "feel" for what makes the business work.

In More Depth

The higher you go in an organization, the more out of touch you can get with what's really happening at the point of greatest impact, the point of contact with the customer. You also lose your feel for the actual operations of your organization, whether they be finance, legal, shipping, telemarketing, or whatever.

Part of that is inevitable. There is not time to be involved with all the details. You do, however, need to keep your feel for what's going on. This takes discipline and an understanding of how important this task is. You will be tempted to slight this aspect because you have "more important things to do."

When you lose touch with your customers or employees, though, you enter a red zone. This danger zone is very well disguised. You often don't see it until you've stepped on a mine, and you ask yourself, "Why didn't I see that coming?" The reason is that you didn't bother to walk through the field and see people laying the mines.

Walk through your operation regularly. Talk with employees and customers (especially those who will tell you the truth and not just what you like to hear). Occasionally, do the job: sell to a customer, pack a shipment, type a memo. It pays in the long run.

The Idea in Action

Sue was the regional manager for a chain of shoe stores. She had worked her way up through sales clerk, store manager, and district manager, to her current position. Although not a college graduate, she was recognized throughout the company for her ability to spot trends and to manage and motivate the work force.

At a national conference, Sue was asked to speak to her colleagues and give them the secrets of her effectiveness.

"I guess I just don't know any better," she started. "I'm not smart enough to figure stuff out myself, so I ask people. I go into the stores and ask the customers what they like and what they don't like. I've even been known to follow people who look in the window and walk away, to ask why they didn't come in. I ask my employees what is working, and is not working, in their jobs and what I can do to make their jobs easier and more productive. I occasionally stock the shelves in a store to find out why the stockers in the store are having problems with a particular display. I also go back to the warehouse one day a year and work with the people in packing and shipping so I can understand how all that works. I'm just too dumb to figure it out myself."

Yeah, dumb like a fox.

For Reflection

When you list all the different functions that you manage or that impact your area of responsibility, in which area is your understanding the weakest?

When was the last time you talked with actual customers? What were the five things they liked least and the five they liked most about your product or service?

What is one problem your employees are experiencing that you could do something about?

52

LISTEN FOR THE UNSPOKEN

Listen for what is not being said and who is not saying it. It is possibly your most valuable piece of information.

In More Depth

You must listen with your heart as well as your ears. Listening is an extremely powerful management tool. Yet, the majority of managers do not know how to listen.

Hearing the words another person speaks is just the first level of listening. Most managers don't even get this far. After the first few words, their minds fill in the rest of the sentence or start formulating a response, not hearing the end of what the other person is saying. Is it surprising that surveys of employee morale have poor communications at the top of the list of management transgressions? At least listen to what a person is saying. There is no need for a less-than-split-second response. Some managers are shocked that other people actually respect them more when they hear them out and take time before responding.

But there is a much more powerful level of listening that involves the heart, mind, and intuition. When you're listening to someone speak, but your heart tells you there is a discrepancy between what they're feeling and what they're saying, remember that as you evaluate the message. Ask them some questions to check out your intuition.

Listen in the larger sense. You will be amazed at what you actually hear.

The Idea in Action

Chiang was owner of a 90-employee food manufacturing firm in New England. He worked hard and tried to be fair to all employees. His operation had grown over 16 years and was fairly profitable. However, he had the feeling things were not "right" in the organization.

He decided to ask some of his employees what they thought. Everyone said things were fine. One said, "Things around here are okay, just like any other business." Another said, "I like you and I like the food industry." A third said, in a very formal and measured manner, "This place works fine; we're not here to be a social club anyway."

Despite the words, Chiang still felt, after these exchanges, that something was wrong in his company. He pondered the conversations. What did the guy mean, "Just like any other business."? Why did the second employee limit her remarks to me and the industry, and not mention her fellow workers? Why was the third so rigid and paced? What was behind the social club remark?

Chiang followed up on what was missing, edited, and biased in the communication. He ultimately discovered severe morale problems that were harming productivity. But only by listening beyond the words was he able to discern the problem and address it.

For Reflection

How often do you stop hearing what someone is saying, filling in the information and formulating a response while they are still talking?

Listen today to someone and answer this: Do you think that person was not saying something, feeling something different, or telling you only what you wanted to hear?

What could you do today to improve your listening?

53

LEARN TO DISAGREE WITHOUT BEING DISAGREEABLE

Feedback and alternative perspectives are essential to a healthy organization. How you present your views will determine how you are perceived by colleagues and employees.

In More Depth

As a leader, on occasion you will need to present alternative opinions and disagree with people. It comes with the job. Certainly you can use the power of your position to bulldoze an opinion through, or you can grandstand. You might even win a few battles with these tactics.

Your long-term effectiveness depends on how you handle disagreement. You can do this easily by focusing your disagreement on the issue, and not on the person with whom you are disagreeing. You may even need to make the distinction by saying something like, "George, I respect you and your work. However, I must disagree with this (decision, process, conclusion), and here is why…"

You will be far more successful if you do not create enemies when you disagree with people. When you create an enemy, that person may spend time, energy, and perhaps money to retaliate. You will probably need to respond, sapping your time, energy, and money from far more important matters.

Do not mistake being nice for being weak. As you go higher in an organization, you will find many nice people. They got there by building relationships, not destroying them, and few would call these people weak.

The Idea in Action

Carla C. was chairperson for the chamber of commerce committee on economic development for the city. She was also president of the board of realtors and owned her own real estate agency. The committee comprised 23 business and civic leaders, many of whom had conflicting opinions and wanted any recommendation to benefit their interests.

Carla recognized these conflicts and the potential danger for her. This would be a very visible position. She was bound to disagree with a number of the members of the committee. She would be faced with doing business personally with many of the members and their organizations, and she certainly would not want to alienate potential clients.

Sure enough, the disagreements materialized. At times, Carla was tempted to attack people she felt were attacking her. Instead, she stayed calm and made her points without being disagreeable. Some key phrases served her well: "I can understand that you have a different opinion on this particular issue." "Let's keep focused on the issue and try to keep personalities out of it."

Yes, she was often frustrated, but she never lost her cool or sacrificed her opinions, although she did allow herself to compromise without feeling her ego was on the line. And in the end, her strong but flexible leadership gained her the respect of all the committee members.

For Reflection

Do you perceive a difference between disagreeing with a person and disagreeing with ideas, statements, and actions? What is it?

List two ways to be less disagreeable when disagreeing with someone?

Have you known someone who was able to disagree without being disagreeable? How did that person do it?

54

HOLD PEOPLE TO THEIR COMMITMENTS

Expect people to honor their agreements, both formal and informal. Not only is it good management, it also calls forth people's integrity.

In More Depth

Imagine the difference in results between two organizations, basically the same except that in one people don't expect (or demand) that others honor their commitments. Agreements are not kept, deadlines are not met, and no one cares enough to change it. In theory, few would disagree with the principle of holding people to their word. In practice, though, it is a stumbling block for many managers. They may object to a major violation of trust, yet let smaller things slide.

When you hold your people to their word, you send a powerful message about leadership to them: You let them know that you value what they say; that you depend on them; that you expect integrity within the organization and in interactions with you; and that you pay attention to closure on any agreement.

Even if there's resistance at first, hold your ground. This may be a new behavior for some people. In the end, respect and trust will prevail. And don't forget, it goes for; you, too.

The Idea in Action

As marketing manager for a computer products firm, Calvin C. was transferred to the western region to revitalize sales efforts there.

An examination of the backgrounds of his salespeople revealed no problem with their education and training. He met them, and they seemed friendly and eager. A review of their work reports showed they were doing what was necessary to achieve sales objectives. So Calvin concluded there must be something different about the region's market that would account for the group's lower productivity.

It took several months to grasp the real problem. When he asked the salespeople to return calls within two hours, they would agree, but when he checked, they would have let the response gap "slip" to four or five hours. When he asked them to make 20 calls per week, they felt 16 was close enough. He asked them to make a few changes in their presentations, and learned later they did not follow through.

Now Calvin knew. The problem was the group's failure to meet commitments. He had lost faith in their word, they had lost trust in each other, and worst of all, customers didn't trust them. They were not bad people. They had just let things slide, but the loss of trust between people, be it boss-employee, employee-employee, or customer-company, is always devastating in the long term.

Calvin began a campaign of holding his reps to their word. If they failed to do it, there were negative consequences. He met some resentment, but eventually his staff grew to respect him. They relearned how to be counted on. They developed trust in each other. Customers developed trust in them again. The change also showed in their monthly sales figures.

For Reflection

How do you hold people to their commitments?
Do you always live up to your word?
What's been your experience in letting people slide a bit in their integrity?

55

BE DIPLOMATIC WITHOUT SACRIFICING THE MESSAGE

Every communication is a chance to empower. Learn when to be blunt, when to soft-pedal, and when to straddle the line.

In More Depth

One of the greatest requirements for your success as a manager or leader is your ability to communicate. You must get your message across, and you must empower the receivers. Whether it is to motivate them to make more sales or stop them from coming in late, you are still "empowering" people to a particular behavior.

You also need to be diplomatic. Deliver your message in such a way that you honor the person receiving it. Honoring means being sensitive to the fact that you are dealing with a feeling human being. It doesn't mean you have to like the person, the message, or what the person stands for.

One key is to avoid extremes. If you're too direct, people tend to tune out. On the other hand, some people lose their audience by being overly diplomatic. This is a critical mistake. It confuses the listener, and you're perceived as a poor communicator.

The Idea in Action

Jill was a fine organizational consultant; so good, in fact, that she formed her own firm. She hired top-quality talent and prepared to take the firm to new heights. Naturally, these people had different talents and temperaments. One associate was a hard-nosed former business executive who believed in straight talk—"Just tell me the facts." Having worked with many corporate executives and leaders, Jill was the consummate diplomat. She knew people listened to her better when they didn't feel attacked and when they felt she was treating them with respect.

In preparing this associate for a meeting with a client, she found herself being run over, as he demanded a short, succinct briefing. She tried to tell him the importance of background information and political sensitivity. Finally, she just said, "Fred, you've got to learn to be more diplomatic. That's all there is to it."

He looked and her and simply said, "Okay." He had his clear message and he was happy. He was, in fact, diplomatic with clients, but in his own interactions he needed his communication to be direct.

On the other end of the spectrum was a junior trainer. Char was obviously very cultivated, great at diplomacy and charm, but she often lost her audiences by qualifying her points too much, such as:"I know it's tough to deal with problem employees, but sometimes you have to find ways to alter their behavior. When you talk with them you need to tell them what needs attention so that they make the necessary alterations."

Jill pointed out the problem and showed her how to hit them between the eyes: "Even though it's sometimes tough to discipline employees, you must tell them to stop behaving inappropriately and remind them what appropriate behavior is."

For Reflection

How diplomatic would you say you are, on a scale of 1 to 10?

Do you know when to modify your delivery to be more direct or less?

Do you always show respect for other people when you talk with them, no matter what the message is? How?

56

HANDLE EMPLOYEE PROBLEMS PROMPTLY

You will have the most impact and get the best results by handling personnel problems immediately. They never get better and it's always more painful to delay.

In More Depth

On rare occasions an employee problem resolves itself without intervention. The key word is "rare." Don't rely on that happening. If you ignore the problem, your staff will see you as ineffective, which could encourage further unproductive behavior. It's like a silent stamp of approval.

If you find yourself reluctant to act, don't feel alone. Most managers dislike this part of the job. Just be calm, review the facts, and make a decision. Having done this, inform anyone directly affected by it and then make sure the decision is enforced.

A final thought. Often the employee problems you see are only symptoms of a greater problem hidden beneath the surface. In these cases, the temptation is to resolve the problem of the moment. Dig deeper. See if the current problem is just one manifestation of something bigger. With good perceptions, questions, and analysis, you may be able to deal with several problems in one stroke.

The Idea in Action

Farrah was the advertising sales manager for a metropolitan newspaper, a highly visible and responsible job with 3 supervisors, 27 salespeople, and 6 support staff reporting to her.

One employee in the national accounts section was notorious for not turning in reports on time, and he frequently argued with his supervisor. In spite of this, he was one of the top performers in the office.

Farrah was relatively new to the job. Her income and bonus depended on producing a high level of revenue for the newspaper, so she was reluctant to deal with this problem employee, fearing he might become even more disruptive, or worse yet, go to work for the competition.

Six months passed, and the guy became even more scornful of accepted procedures, and the relationship with his supervisor was now very adversarial. Farrah's joking comments to the troublemaker were too oblique. They didn't work. Moreover, other employees were now starting to get lax and rebellious.

Farrah could ignore it no longer. She called the salesperson into her office and told him his behavior was not acceptable, outlined what was, and asked him if he could accept that. To her surprise, he said yes. He did say, however, that everybody felt the reports were time consuming and unproductive, but were afraid to speak out.

She investigated his claim and did, in fact, modify the reporting system. The salesperson held up his end of the bargain. On the one occasion where he threatened to relapse, she just reminded him of their agreement.

For Reflection

What employee problem have you been hoping would go away?

What is your pattern in handling employee problems?

Thinking back to the last employee problem you handled, is it possible that it was only a symptom and not the real problem?

57

TERMINATE WHEN NECESSARY

Counsel them to leave, if possible. If not, terminate cleanly and quickly.

In More Depth

Firing people is unpleasant. It is, however, sometimes necessary. If you don't do it when you know you should (and you know), the problem always gets worse and you will be forced to do it under even more unpleasant circumstances. By the way, your employees also know who should be fired. It's rarely a surprise.

Before firing, try counseling the person to leave the organization. Ask how he or she sees the company's goals and activities, and how he or she fits in. Say honestly that you don't see a good fit, and give specifics. Do talk with your human resources (HR) people or attorneys to make sure you do everything legally, but remember, you're the boss. They are your advisers. The decision is yours.

When you must terminate, do it quickly and cleanly. Bring the employee in. Tell that person his or her services are no longer needed. Say why, briefly and clearly. Explain any severance procedures. Dismiss the person. Be professional and sensitive, but don't get into a debate or prolong the process. This is a very awkward time for both parties, certainly not the time to develop a friendship.

The Idea in Action

Juanita R. was the manager of the research department of a large defense contractor. She had an employee who had received low performance ratings, did not respond to an action plan for improvement, and was hurting the operations of her department. The other employees were complaining about him.

She knew he needed to be fired. Though kind and fair, Juanita could be tough when necessary, but like most managers, she procrastinated. The employee only continued to aggravate her, causing morale to drop among other employees and weakening their perception of Juanita's abilities.

Finally, an incident occurred that made immediate dismissal imperative. After checking with human resources on the severance procedure, she called him into her office. Juanita knew she should get right to the point, tell him of his dismissal early in the conversation, tell him specifically why, inform him of the process, and end the discussion.

Instead, she experienced a bout of guilt and tried to soften the blow by telling him she appreciated the good things he had done and how she liked him personally. He then began to object to the decision, defending his overall performance—using her own words—made a direct appeal to her friendship—again quoting her—and insisted he be retained.

She got through it, but that evening, as she was drinking her Maalox, Juanita vowed forever after to follow the simple rules for termination and never again let it get drawn out and messy.

For Reflection

Is there anyone in your organization who should be terminated? How would your employees answer this question?

What do you need to do to initiate the process of terminating this person?

If not yet at the critical dismissal stage, could you counsel this person to leave the organization without having to resort to termination

Image

58

APPEARANCE REALLY DOES COUNT

The way you dress, groom, and carry yourself, along with your personal habits, can enhance or doom your chances to succeed.

In More Depth

While it seems that your knowledge of the job and your competency to perform it should be all that matter, that's not reality. The way you present yourself can be just as important, perhaps more so.

Marketers know that packaging often spells the success or failure of a product. Think of a grocery store where the best quality food, let's say bread, is packaged unattractively—worn or torn or a bit too large—and displayed haphazardly. Will that product command a premium price? Will it even be purchased?

The same applies to a person who wants to progress (or be hired) in an organization. Package yourself well and you may at least be taken off the shelf for consideration. It's simple. Here's how.

Wear good, proper-fitting clothing. If you aren't good at picking clothes, find someone who is and ask for help. Try to be in fashion. Have a professional hairstyle. Always give the appearance of being clean and fresh. Keep your shoes shined. Bathe often so there is never any body odor and use toothpaste and mouthwash. To go a step further, practice good posture, improve your speaking voice, brush up on etiquette, or take a class in wine appreciation.

Common sense? Yes. But we all know someone who violates these rules and who, because of it, is not taken seriously for better jobs.

The Idea in Action

Joel was a smart and talented student in the business school of a major university—good grades, good personality, involved in extracurricular activities. Despite all this, he belonged to the "who-cares-what-I-look-like" school of grooming. Upon graduation, it came time to get a job. Joel knew enough to go to the barber and buy a suit for interviews, and he landed work easily. On the job, he figured he didn't have to wear a "stupid" suit anymore. He seldom polished his shoes and his hair was unruly. But he did good work.

Over the next year and a half, two students hired at the same time he was were promoted to the next level. Joel was baffled. While they were competent, he felt no doubt his work was better. He asked his boss what he was doing wrong. "You do good work," came the reply. "But you don't impress people as someone ready for management. Your appearance is sloppy. Management thinks that might translate into sloppy work. The higher you go, the more you have to represent the company to people, and your grooming is not the image the company wants."

The advice was timely. With, good clothes and grooming and good business etiquette, Joel was back on track within six months and continues on the career course he always envisioned for himself.

For Reflection

How would others rate your wardrobe and grooming (your packaging)?
What could you do to improve your packaging?
How can you guide employees jobs to realize the need for a positive appearance?

59

SEX AND WORK DON'T MIX

Romantic involvement at work causes problems. It impairs your judgment, exposes you to legal problems, and undermines team respect.

In More Depth

A romantic fantasy about someone at work is generally harmless enough. But if fantasy gives way to action, there can be problems.

When you're romantically involved, you tend to see only the positive, and overlook things you normally wouldn't. Even worse for a manager is to promote or in some way elevate the career of someone he or she is involved with. If, in the euphoria, you misjudge the person's qualifications, you may have to live with resulting problems for a long time. Besides, have you ever known lovers who didn't fight? How will that affect the workplace? How will it affect your performance?

Then there are the legal problems. In our litigious society, even innocent flirting has resulted in large financial settlements and ruined careers. The "consenting adults" defense virtually disappears in manager-subordinate cases, especially if the subordinate claims to have felt pressured.

Finally, workplace dalliances can cause resentment, impede working relationships, and lead other employees to lose respect for the parties involved. They may feel—understandably—that the special person is receiving preferential treatment. And if you've ever wondered whether employees know if the boss is having an affair, assume they do.

The Idea in Action

Jack was the divisional manager of a manufacturing firm. A support person, Arleen, often worked on projects that required working evenings and weekends with him. Jack found Arleen attractive and she seemed receptive to his attention. One evening they decided to have a drink together. One thing lead to another and they began having an affair.

Though Jack and Arleen were very discreet at work, it became obvious to other employees—the little glances, the knowing smiles, the little tidbits they seemed to know about each other. Then Jack started taking Arleen's side in little disputes. Resentment started to build and the innuendo mill went to work.

Then a promotional opportunity arose that Arleen wanted, as did several other employees. Arleen was good at her work but not exceptionally qualified for the new job. Now Jack felt he was in the middle of a minefield. She wanted his support, but sensed his hesitancy. They fought. She threatened a sexual harassment suit. He panicked and gave her the job.

Later, when they split, he was faced not only with an angry employee who had forced his hand, but also with other employees who felt the tension and resented it. Their productivity diminished. Since Jack's chances for advancement depended on the performance of his division, his future is on hold.

For Reflection

Are you thinking about "crossing the line" into an office romance?

Can any of your actions be construed as a romantic gesture or sexual harassment?

Have you realistically considered the possible consequences of an office romance?

60

TAKE CARE OF YOURSELF

Be responsible for your physical and mental health, your social life, your spiritual life, your finances—in a word, your entire well-being—both on and off the job.

In More Depth

For peak efficiency, take care of yourself. For fun and happiness in your life, take care of yourself. Certainly, honor your body with exercise and good food, but there's more to it than just proper diet and getting some exercise.

Take time to relax; great ideas flow from a relaxed mind. Take time to play; it renews you and gives a valuable perspective on life. Spend time enjoying family and friends; they offer you a foundation, support, and joy.

Get in touch with your spiritual side, whether it's based in religion, metaphysics, nature, or even art. Find that part of yourself that touches something bigger than you are, and connects you with all of life.

Put your affairs in order: finances, wills, legal issues, old resentments, unfulfilled dreams, and private wishes.

Do all of this and your life will be balanced, fulfilled, and despite the time it takes away from work, extremely productive.

The Idea in Action

Mr. Aban was a successful attorney—in fact, principal in a firm which bore his name. Known as a fine attorney and boss, he often devoted 12-hour days and weekends to his practice.

He did this for 19 years. Then he began to notice his energy and interest dropping. His home life was not the greatest and his health was marginal (he liked several donuts in the morning, high-fat fast food for lunch, and elaborate dinners with clients nearly every night). He had no time for exercise.

One Sunday morning, he felt pains in his chest and was rushed to the hospital—mild heart attack. Mr. Aban was a smart man. He got the message.

With the determination he always showed in his law practice, he set about getting his life in order. Out went the potato chips. He and his wife began walking every morning and evening. They even talked again and discovered they still loved each other. He spent time with his son, who felt like he had a father again. He also renewed friendships he had all but forgotten.

He took care of problems that had been developing, including updating his own will (you know the old story about taking care of everyone else first). And, very important, he recovered his spiritual values, which provided him a serenity he had not known for years.

Did all these life changes detract from his law practice? On the contrary, he was brilliant in the courtroom now, as he was rested and had time to think about new approaches and refine some old ones. His colleagues enjoyed working with him more, which improved team spirit. And he even found new sources of clients in the health club he joined and in the little retreat community he and his wife had started visiting.

For Reflection

Honestly, how balanced is your life?

What two aspects of your life need the most attention? Where are you overdoing it?

What stops you from taking better care of yourself?

61

FIT IN, BUT DON'T BE INVISIBLE

Being too different is the kiss of death. Being a clone may mean never being seen or heard. Try to strike a balance.

In More Depth

To be an effective manager and to succeed careerwise means balancing between being visible and being out-of-step. There is an unwritten organizational code that values team playing and stability. Never forget this, even if the corporate image makers also claim to value originality, diversity, and innovation. The trick is to correctly determine the parameters of acceptable behavior (often unwritten and uncommunicated) and avoid violating them.

You *can* be an individual. In fact, you should feel comfortable exercising unique aspects of your personality. Establishing a reputation for excellence almost by definition involves using the very traits that can get you into trouble if carried too far—originality and innovation.

For beginning managers, the temptation to emulate other successful managers is almost irresistible. That's fine. You can learn valuable behaviors that way. Still, at some point you must distinguish yourself from the crowd. Agree when appropriate, but don't fear to disagree. Use proven techniques, but don't be afraid to try informed experiments. Maximize your strengths, and exploit your magic. This strategy will serve your career and inspire your team. People like to be associated with a winner. They want their leaders to *lead*.

The Idea in Action

Gregory was promoted to branch manager of a major bank. He was sharp, had strong career ambitions, and was respected. Since there were many other branch managers, Gregory felt he would need to be aggressive in his approach to be considered for future promotions.

He set out to make his team the best branch in the chain. He changed the way everyone worked with customers, including having staff members call customers to determine their level of satisfaction. He even set up coffee for customers waiting in line. Gregory's imaginative practices set him apart. His future looked bright.

Then he grew a bit cocky. At executive peer meetings, his behavior bordered on overbearing—touting his successful techniques, being flippant in his presentations, even telling others how they should do things. Finally, at a branch manager meeting, a fed-up VP became annoyed enough to speak up: "You're a good manager, Gregory. Your ideas have worked very well at your branch, but they are not necessarily for everyone. I am getting concerned about your ability to fit in as part of our larger effort. You're marching to your own drummer.

This outpouring shook Gregory to his foundation and forced him to take a personal and private inventory. He had to face up to having overstepped the bounds of propriety, and despite his successes, he was in danger of losing his place on the team.

For Reflection

What are you doing to stand out from the crowd?

What does a corporate clone look like in your company? Do you fit that description?

What are the "real" boundaries for originality within your organization?

62
YOU ARE NOT PERFECT

Perfection is rarely if ever required. Both you and your employees will make mistakes. This is part of being human.

In More Depth

Many leaders feel they have to convey an image of perfection. They fear they'll lose respect if they admit to any weakness. That's not true. While everyone loves a hero, few expect perfection. The important thing is to minimize mistakes and learn from them. Management is truly the art of dealing with people, who are by nature imperfect. You will be a much better leader if you accept that you and your employees will make mistakes. As a bonus, you will be much healthier emotionally.

The problem with wanting to maintain a perfect image is that people know it's false. It breeds the attitude in employees that they cannot admit mistakes either and leads to two destructive behaviors. Some hide their mistakes, a potential disaster for a business. Others fear doing anything that would cause them to make a mistake in the first place, another long-term loss in productivity and creativity.

You need not publicly confess every error you make. Just be aware of your humanity. Your employees will actually respect you more when they know that you know that you are human too.

The Idea in Action

Danny L. retired from the military and became the chief of security at a state university. He was a strong personality and a dominating manager.

When Dan took the position, he simply kept existing policies and practices in place but enforced them more rigorously. This worked until the university did an operational audit of security policies and procedures and found they needed updating in light of new legal, social, and political considerations.

Danny was assigned to design and implement the new policies and procedures. He had no experience in this, but rather than admit to this he decided to do it himself anyway.

Once he had written them up, he required the new rules be enforced as rigorously as the old ones. When some concerns were voiced, Danny dug in. He didn't like anyone questioning his decisions.

More problems with the new rules began to surface. Some were difficult to administer. Others were borderline illegal. Still, Danny defended them vehemently. He could not admit to any mistake. Even when a member of the administration expressed serious legal concerns and employees demonstrated how several procedures were virtually impossible to enforce, he continued to insist that they be enforced.

In the end, everyone acknowledged a mistake had been made. Danny's reputation declined along with the department's. The specific problems would have been easy to change if only he could have admitted to human imperfection. Danny's stress level rose to the point that he ultimately had to leave on a stress disability claim.

For Reflection

How do you feel about being seen as less than perfect?
Do any of your employees feel they are above making mistakes?
How do you deal with employees who hate to admit their imperfections?

63

SUPERIOR MANAGEMENT REQUIRES PROFESSIONAL DEVELOPMENT

Never stop learning. Management is a profession, not a right or inheritance. Accept that there will frequently be things you don't know and that finding better ways to do things is part of the job.

In More Depth

Doctors must attend seminars and workshops to update their credentials. CPAs must continue their education to maintain certification...as do teachers. Lawyers must constantly update themselves on the ever-changing legal scene.

Many managers, though, seem to think the promotion into management or getting an MBA means they are finished with their education. No.

Developing and maintaining superior management skills is a lifelong quest. You must read books and journals, take courses, attend seminars and workshops, and learn from other professionals. We are experiencing very rapid change in management practices as well as in the organizational environment. You must continue to keep yourself up to date, not only for your future success, but for your survival as a manager.

The Idea in Action

Ten years ago, Donald P. was an up-and-coming MBA graduate. He knew all the textbook answers. Hired by a Fortune 500 company, he soon had to learn how to convert all the theory into practical applications. It took several years to make the transition to practicing manager, but he did very well at it. He had received two promotions and was well respected.

One day, sitting in a meeting, a sense of doom rolled over him. All the other managers seemed so much more in touch with new techniques and were bringing more new ideas to the table than he was. Unbelievable as it was, he couldn't remember the last book he'd read on his field. He subscribed to the journals but never got around to them, and his membership in trade groups was for show only. He was bored.

Rather than scrap all the years he had devoted to his company and field, he decided to attend a seminar he had noticed called "Career Revitalization." What did he have to lose? At the seminar, he soon realized most of the attendees were burned out, just like him. The trainers covered a lot of suggestions, from changing careers to taking measures to make your current career more challenging and more enjoyable. Among the measures discussed were getting back in touch with the latest trends.

Donald was intrigued enough to follow up. An article in one of his publications caught his eye. It referenced a book that he ordered and read. This, led him to enroll in a three-day workshop on managerial skills for the nineties. A few weeks later, Donald was gratified to hear himself contributing fresh ideas in his divisional meetings and speaking knowledgably. He had discovered that one of the secrets to getting ahead is a simple matter that you can control yourself and your training.

For Reflection

What are you doing to keep current in your profession?
What are you doing to learn new concepts and ideas?
Honestly, are you keeping up?

64
ALWAYS DO WELL

Your reputation will follow you. People will assume the same behavior in all your dealings.

In More Depth

Always do well whatever you do. It's better to limit your activities and do them well than to do a mediocre job at many things. Too many people think "padding out their résumés is the way to get ahead: sitting on different boards, volunteering for lots of committees, accepting yet another project. How much a person works is that person's business, but nothing is gained if you end up doing nothing really well.

An alternative approach is to choose your involvement carefully and commit yourself to producing quality results at anything you lend you name to. Don't worry. You'll get noticed. In fact, you'll get to pick the cream from an abundance of opportunities.

Think of it this way: To be a truly outstanding boss, just consistently do everything 10 percent better than other people. You'd establish a fine reputation just by doing that.

The Idea in Action

May Ling had passed the bar exam and was proud to be the first lawyer in her family. She was determined to be a success in the law firm that recruited her. She was willing to work hard, and her goal was to become a senior partner. The night before she was to begin at the law firm, she shared dinner with her aunt, a woman known for her wisdom despite having had little formal education.

May Ling told her aunt of her dreams and how she was going to get involved in everything so she could "learn it all"; and she was going to get involved in the community so she could establish contacts and bring in business so that the firm would consider her for a promotion; and she would take an advanced course at night to become a specialist. The old woman sat her ambitious niece down and gave her this advice: "Be good at whatever you do, and do only what you are willing to do well."

May Ling was a bit disappointed that her aunt didn't encourage her in the more rigorous course. Her advice seemed so simple and uninspired. Her aunt had always given such good advice. This was the first time she had ever been disappointed.

That night, she had trouble sleeping. She kept thinking about her aunt's words and the old woman's lack of education. Had the world finally passed by her eminent forebear? Did she not understand how a powerful lawyer worked? Still, the simple wisdom resonated in her mind.

May Ling decided to go with her gut instinct and follow her aunt's advice (even if she did harbor some doubts about its simplicity). Ms. Kim, Esq., senior law partner, now tells her new law interns this story and advises them to follow her wise aunt's advice.

For Reflection

Make a list of all your involvements. Are you doing everything well?

What should you give up in order to concentrate on those activities to which you are truly committed?

If you could start from zero today, what projects, activities, and involvements would you choose to do (and do well)?

About the Authors

BRUCE HYLAND is a West Coast consultant in organizational development who has worked with organizations ranging from K mart and Payless Shoes to the city governments of Palm Springs and Oakland, California. A former executive with American Express, he lectures widely on organizational and human resources development and teaches at City College of San Francisco.

MERLE YOST is a specialist in organizational development and psychology. He has worked as a consultant with for-profit and not-for-profit organizations alike, including Southland Corporation, the March of Dimes, and the Muscular Dystrophy Association. He is currently an associate of The Center for Human Relations in Oakland, California.